The Essential Buyer's Guide
LANCIA
DELTA HF 4WD & INTEGRALE
1986 to 1994

Your marque expert:
Paul Baker

VELOCE PUBLISHING
THE PUBLISHER OF FINE AUTOMOTIVE BOOKS

www.veloce.co.uk

First published in December 2020 by Veloce Publishing Limited, Veloce House, Parkway Farm Business Park, Middle Farm Way, Poundbury, Dorchester DT1 3AR,
England. Tel +44 (0)1305 260068 / Fax 01305 250479 / e-mail info@veloce.co.uk / web www.veloce.co.uk or www.velocebooks.com.
ISBN:978-1-787115-38-5; UPC: 6-36847-01538-1.

Introduction

Let's turn the clock back to 1986. Lancia had suffered the double blow of the deaths of Henri Toivonen and Sergio Cresto on the 1986 Tour De Corse rally, and then Group B was cancelled. This resulted in the S4 programme being short-lived; therefore, Lancia needed a fast and successful replacement for the S4, so very little time was given to produce a successful Group A car in the new series as well as a homologated road version.

Esteemed engineers Sergio Limone, Bruno Cena and Giorgio Pianta set out to complete this task in a short timeframe, which they achieved, and the HF 4WD was born. The road car was the byproduct of this incredible car, and, as time passed, the car evolved each year to produce first the 8v Integrale in 1988, then the 16v Integrale in 1989, followed by the HF integrale (Evo I or Deltona) in 1991, and finally the HF integrale Evo II Cat (Deltona) in 1993.

Importantly, this was a car first and foremost designed for winning rallies: road use came second. It is, of course, more usual for a rally car to be developed from a road car. The Lancia marketing department, along with the vision and support of Ing Vittorio Ghidella, realised that if this car was to succeed in world rallying then sales of the road car would naturally increase. The rally version was a world champion, and became so with aplomb, winning six consecutive championships, the most successful rally car to date.

So, let's be clear, if you are considering buying into this amazing world, here is a warning: it will bite you, and there is no way back once you have been

The Lancia production line at the Chivasso factory in Italy, taken during a Lancia Motor Club trip in 1994.

bitten! Even today, these cars are a joy to drive for the enthusiastic driver, they are communicative, fluid, capable and very useable and practical.

Thanks

My thanks go to my friends Alessandro Sopetti, Sergio Limone, Bruno Cena, Enrico Masala, Paolo Buffardi, Vittorio Roberti, Giovanni & Elio Baldi, Domenico Fasano, Roberto Cassetta, Peter Collins, John Whalley, Rodolfo Gaffino Di Rossi, Roberto Franco, and, sadly, two late friends Marcello Minerbi and Giorgio Pianta. Without their help, guidance, and experiences they shared with me this book would not be possible and the Lancia Delta story would not have been such a passionate love for me.

Thanks to Neil Boggas, Tanc Barrett and Justin Narillo for pictures of the Dealers Collection edition. Pictures supplied by Peter Collins are credited as such, the remaining photographs are from the author's personal collection.

Thanks also to my wife Gemma, who has immersed herself into this world, and has embraced my enthusiasm.

Contents

The Essential Buyer's Guide™ currency
At the time of publication a BG unit of currency "●" equals approximately
£1.00/US$1.31/Euro 1.11. Please adjust to suit current exchange rates.

1 Is it the right car for you?
– marriage guidance

Tall and short drivers

The Delta was designed by Giugiaro, the Italian designer who was responsible for the VW Golf. The driving position is upright, giving a sense of involvement and immediacy with great visibility. The front seats give excellent side support due to the side bolsters, and earlier cars have extra slide out supports that give additional support to the knee area. There is also a handy passenger grab handle for comfort and stability when travelling on the more 'exciting' roads. Most drivers will fit comfortably in a Delta, regardless of size, as it resembles a straightforward hatchback (although 6ft plus rear seat passengers may have limited headroom).

Weight of controls

The steering is perfectly weighted, fluid, and not over-assisted. However, it is important to state that a right-hand drive conversion may lessen the driving experience, due to the substituted parts that were used.

Will it fit in the garage?

Take a look at the charts at the end of the book for size: integrales got longer and wider as they evolved. The HF 4WD did not have extended wheelarches, but the 8V integrale and 16v versions had wheelarch extensions added. The Evo models had even wider wheelarches, though these were complete wings rather than extensions, and are the widest of the range.

Interior space

For a performance car of its time, the interior space is comparable to a Golf, but

Standard 8v & 16v integrale interior.

it is faster than most sports cars, with mid-size hatchback space and practicality. Visibility is excellent, although bear in mind extra caution is required on approach to roundabouts due to being left-hand drive. Rear legroom is generous and the back seat experience is comfortable. There are generous sized door pockets on front doors, and the front seats also have handy elasticated storage pockets. There is a generously-sized lockable compartment on the passenger side. Front windows are electrically operated and rear windows are manually operated. In the central console there is a headlamp adjustment wheel.

Luggage capacity
With a well-shaped rear hatchback and folding rear seats, there is ample luggage space, with only the space saver wheel and tyre encroaching on the left-hand side of the hatch.

Usability
A standard integrale is as docile as any hot hatchback to drive around town, suburbs and country roads, with the suspension being on the side of firm. There is an extremely impressive amount of grip that is far beyond most cars of this type, giving it great capability in all weathers under normal driving conditions. Those who do push the boat out further, and are fully prepared for the acceleration, grip and braking, will find it better than any other car of its time; it is very predictable and communicative, unlike many supercars. You can also see out of it!

The integrale's ergonomics are not as good as the best high volume cars of its time, they are slightly quirky; however, one day spent driving this car and you will realise that there are gauges for everything, which make life simple and tell you exactly what is going on with the car. Importantly, there are gauges for oil pressure and oil temperature; a feature that most manufacturers have not found necessary to add, which I find most surprising, as they are really useful. Some magazines have described the instruments as confusing, but in my experience the truth is the exact opposite. Fuel consumption can be frightening when the available performance is used to its full potential, or on long motorway journeys. However, fuel consumption is not extreme in normal driving conditions in spite of a shape that is not slippery, a four-wheel-drive system and large tyres. The integrale can be durable, and is better than other earlier Italian makes that have a reputation for poor electrics or high oil consumption; that is not the case with this car so long as you adhere to service routines.

Parts availability
Good club and expert support from specialists is essential, and although some parts are expensive and hard to find, generally, with a little patience and help, most parts can be tracked down. Some of the car is standard hatchback, and there is sometimes a crossover to Fiat and Alfa parts.

Service costs
If you are comparing it to a Supercar it is much less costly, but for a hatchback it may be considered expensive, as the car is quite complicated. The basic budget per annum depends on mileage and use; however you must include, every two to three years, around ⬤1k for maintenance, to include tyres, a major belt service, which

should cost around ●800-900 including parts, and add the same for the clutch and water pump (it's a good idea to do both together).

Insurance
Today there are several schemes available, some attractively priced through the Lancia Motor club, offering various policies that consider low mileage. Now that the car is a classic there are a lot more schemes to be found, and agreed values are important on these cars. Some offer track day use, which can be beneficial if you plan to go on track. Consider the replacement cost; how and where would you find a similar example, and how much would it cost? Always shop around, but get the best cover you can. Windscreen cover is also important. Always use a reputable insurer, and check your policy. Cheap can be for a reason!

Investment potential
This car is extremely investable; and it is also now sometimes being rediscovered by new collectors of a different age in new markets. The values of all versions of the integrale are likely to increase, none more so than the limited editions. There are some golden rules to go by (discussed later) and if you stick to these your purchase should go well.

Foibles
For the type of performance available, the integrale has its eccentricities and may not be as predictable as something like a VW Golf, but the driving experience far outweighs this predictability, providing a truly memorable driving experience. It still stands alone, even today, as one of the best all round all weather machines.

Positive points
Buy the right car and you will never regret it, the integrale is as good today as it was when it was made; a joyful driving experience, you can utilise all the power at your disposal when needed, it's amazing on country roads, and has great stopping power, awesome steering, handling, poise and balance in a practical hatchback design, with purposeful looks, rally inspired pedigree, Italian charm and soul, rarity, sublime engine flexibility and smoothness. When driving you will notice you only get good feedback and positive reactions from others of all ages. Firstly, the whole reason you want to have one of these cars is that it steers with pin-like accuracy, handles and grips exceedingly well, brakes without fading, has performance readily available when needed. A good example should show all these traits, if any of these are missing, you have to find out why. The older versions are more subtle and don't stand out too much in a crowd, plus it's a very good family and shopping car. Nothing else compares in the classic market with the sort of performance, practicality and exclusivity.

Negative points
The car was designed a long time ago now, and the body shape is boxy as this was the trending style in the early '80s, but it has aged well, and evolved into a more aggressive animal. The interior features are also dated, with no intermittent rear wiper, a lack of good ventilation, the ride is harsh on poorly surfaced roads, there are bad earths on electrics which can surface (but nothing too serious); the interior can make a rattle or squeak. Evo brakes make an annoying squeal when warm, this

is a design fault that you can rectify by applying Copperslip, but unfortunately it may return.

Alternatives

For space, choose any hatchback; for performance any Supercar; however, for poise, grip, sheer drivability and practicality there is virtually nothing that can compare. Possible alternatives could be:

• Lancia Dedra integrale – Heavier, not a hatch, has four doors, very rare, comparatively cheap, more difficult to import.
• Ford Sapphire Cosworth – Heavier, not a hatch but has four doors.
• Subaru WRX STi – Not a hatch, not as communicative.
• Mitsubishi EVO – Not a hatch.
• Ford Escort Cosworth – Only two doors, not as communicative.
• Audi Quattro – Only two doors, heavier, not as communicative.
• Ford Sierra Cosworth – Only two doors, not as communicative, heavier, only two-wheel drive.

A very well looked after and treasured 8v integrale. (Courtesy Peter Collins)

2 Cost considerations
– affordable, or a money pit?

The cars are now sought after across the globe, and have recently become available for import to the USA. Americans who followed the rally teams and wished to own a homologation special can now do so, due to the 25-year importation laws, so buyers can now afford to buy and import one of the cars which were previously unavailable to them. However, this market is now increasing, and many US-based buyers are reaching out to Europe and Japan to satisfy the demand.

Generally, cars coming from Japan have been maintained to a good standard, but buying from this market does not mean in all cases that the car is better or worth paying more money for than a European equivalent. Japanese specification cars that were imported directly when new had subtle differences, such as different indicator repeaters on the front wings next to a special HF badge for this market only, or later versions of the car being fitted with 16V headlamps. In my experience 80% of the cars coming from Japan have been modified. This includes items such as pedals, hoses, steering wheel, gearlever, etc, which have been personalised by their previous owner – but it is preferable to find a car in its original condition. These modifications do not add value, and make the car less desirable. Cars from Japan may be cheaper than other markets, can have good maintenance history and are more solid in the bodywork.

European market cars are generally the best to buy. Italy has more supply, however its prices tend to be higher. German cars tend to be either well looked after standard cars, or heavily modified examples. You should be aware that there are some Swiss market examples which differ mechanically from other market cars and have less powerful engines.

Press shot of an Evo I model.

Purchase price

There is a large difference in prices, depending on condition, modifications, history and model type. See Chapter 4 for the relative values of the different models. Always get the best car for your budget, while taking into consideration the running costs and potential repairs or restoration work required.

Running costs

Tyres are high-performance, and should be the best you can buy. This applies to all of the running gear. The tyre wear rate can vary from normal to heavy, depending on your driving style and the setup of the car. If setup is incorrect tyres will wear out extremely quickly and fuel consumption will increase.

A gently driven integrale, routinely serviced will be relatively normal in terms of cost to run for the size of car.

Basic budget per annum depends on mileage and use (see chapter 1 for service costs).

Parts prices

Fuel filter	x 12.50 (all)
Fuel pump	x 80 (all)
Sparkplugs	x 3.50-4.50 each
Cambelt	x 14.00-17.50
Balancer shaft belt	x 27.50
Water pump	x 56
Front shock absorber	x 130-150
Rear shock absorber	x 130-150
Front pads	x 36-49 set standard spec
Rear pads	x 20-40 set standard spec
Front disc	x 35-45 each standard spec
Rear disc	x 15-25 each standard spec
Bonnet (only used or NOS available)	Expensive! Perhaps x 1000 used
Front grille frame	x 180
Front door (only used or NOS available)	Expensive! Perhaps x 150 used
Door seal	Not available
Tailgate (only used or NOS available)	Expensive! Perhaps x 250
Windscreen	x 185 bronze or blue.
Tail light lens only	x 42.50
Headlamps individual replacement units	x 70-175 each

3 Living with an integrale

– will you get along together?

Because the integrale is a four-door volume hatchback it is relatively easy to live with. If you live in a right-hand drive market the general driving experience will take a little getting used to, but it is not nearly as challenging as some may have you believe. There are advantages to left-hand drive, such as it being easier to step out onto the kerb without opening the door into oncoming traffic. You will have to get used to the occasional electrical glitch, which is generally down to a poor earth. You will also need to get used to replacing rose joints and anti-roll bar bushes, and keeping an eye on your tyre wear. You may get an expensive repair bill if the transmission or differentials fail, but engines do not leak or consume oil, and as long as maintenance is adhered to they are generally bullet proof. There is no getting away from the fact that this car is mechanically complex, but that's typical of this type of car, and you can mitigate against it by fastidious servicing and preventative maintenance. Your insurance bills may be higher, but as the integrale is now a classic car there are many companies that provide good cover for a reasonable premium.

Good points

Driving from A to B across country there are few cars that will do it as quickly and comfortably as an integrale. It will get you there very safely, with great grip, four wheel drive traction and sound brakes, and the visibility is good. Even bad weather is not a problem. The experience is so communicative and progressive; it is just, simply put, a joy to drive. And yet around town it is also a practical and enjoyable car to drive. The car gives a comfortable enough ride, but it covers distance exceptionally well. It carries anything you would want to carry in a normal family car. As homologation specials go, the styling is purposeful, so it doesn't look unfashionable, but it always turns heads. The driving position is upright, you sit quite high, with a good throw of gearlever, the pedals are well spaced for heel and toe changes, the steering wheel is adjustable for height, and the seat and back rest adjust from front to back.

The Lancia bodyshell is a design penned by Giugiaro for the Delta in late 1970s. It has the practicality of being a hatchback, with four doors, and it seats four comfortably (although 6ft plus rear seat passengers may have limited headroom); it has reasonable sized load area; although it is by today's terms a small car, it is not very wide (Evo versions more so) and is short in length, which means there will not be an issue parking in spaces or a normal sized garage. It is ideal for short trips and weekends away.

Bad points

The car is not very aerodynamic, so for long trips on motorways the fuel consumption is quite high, more so if you are on boost a lot of the time. It is not a light car and has 4WD; the fuel tank is 57 litres so not so large. Generally speaking, it is not the most frugal of cars, but do not forget this is a high-performance vehicle.

As the car was born left-hand drive (and in my opinion should stay that way – more of that topic later) you will have to get used to sitting on the left, so you are closest to the curbside; although easier for parallel parking, and the door opening onto the curbside, you also have to line up the car using a slightly different mindset on the road; you are aware of how close you can be to parked cars and the curb. On roundabouts, visibility can be compromised as you have to look inside the passenger window, and then around the 'A pillar' in the corner of the windscreen to see your entry point, as the A Pillar can hide a vehicle entering to your right.

Overtaking is not a real issue, you can look down the inside of the vehicle you want to overtake, and pass when safe to do so, taking care of your right mirror which also has a blind spot. The car has enough power on boost to get past most things quickly and in a safe way, however, being a passenger on the right side is a daunting experience for some, and I know of quite a number of people who sold their car, or had conversions completed just for this reason.

The car is at its best handling, cornering, braking and steering with pin sharp preciseness, communicating where you are all the time on the road, this experience is diluted gravely with RHD converted examples, as they were completed by now closed businesses (Mike Spence of Reading who did the early examples, and John Whalley of Bishops Stortford who did later conversions), using a Delta HF Turbo pedal box, dashboard, and a FIAT Regatta diesel steering rack which affected the sharpness of the steering; the brake pipes had double the length of travel which affected the immediacy of the brake use as well as the feel. The value and potential investment of a converted car is never going to be the same as an original LHD example.

On long journeys, the seats can cause the driver to get some muscle cramp in the legs or backside due to the high bolsters.

Try to make the car as secure as possible as it is a potential target for thieves, always park it front end in as it is not so obvious that way in public areas. The interior features are also dated, with no intermittent rear wiper, a lack of good ventilation, the ride is harsh on poorly surfaced roads, there are bad earths on electrics which can surface, but nothing too serious; the interior can make a rattle or squeak. Evo brakes make an annoying squeal when warm, this is a design fault you can rectify with applying Copperslip, but unfortunately it may return.

Suspension is rose-jointed, and front anti-roll bar droplinks wear out fast,

Anti rollbar bushes.

Integrale droplinks.

Evo rose joints.

earlier versions have bushes, and these can be changed for items made from dynatrol, which lasts longer. Tyre wear is quick if geometry setup is wrong, 2nd and 3rd gear synchro can wear with harsh use; turbos can wear if the car is not warmed up correctly and allowed to cool down correctly, or if it has low oil quantity/quality/viscosity.

Usability/reliability
In my opinion the most impressive aspect of these cars is their usability in all weathers, thanks to the fantastic steering, which is pin sharp. The steering is perfectly weighted, with acute chassis balance and robustness, brake feel and potency, the power of the engine being used to its potential 90% of the time, and the fluency of all these things working in harmony, which in my opinion is still one of the best driving experiences available at any price.

If well maintained the car is very reliable, but do not ignore the schedules, especially for things like cambelt changes, drive belts, gear selection, clutch use and operation, oil changes, filters, gearbox oil levels, etc. The cars do not use oil, but you must maintain the right level. Maintenance should be done by recommended specialists who know the car well; it is quite complex, needing specialist tools and knowledge, and there is limited space under the bonnet. The Lampredi-designed engine, if looked after, is almost bulletproof: it needs maintenance, but if heeded, should last. It doesn't use oil, or have inherent issues, and the turbos last longer if you get them up to temperature before boosting hard, and let them cool again before switching off the engine. The cars come on boost relatively quickly, and with later Evo models, there is an over-boost that allows for longer boost under acceleration.

Performance
The entire range of cars has very good performance even by today's standards.

The HF 4WD (165bhp), 8v integrale (185bhp), 16v (200bhp), Evo I (210bhp) and Evo II Cat (215bhp), all have their own characteristics depending on the power available. In my opinion, the best is probably the 16v integrale, as it has a usable 200bhp, but weighs less than the Evo models with more power. It is much more of a raw experience than the Evo models which feel more relaxing to drive.

Car magazine tested the Evo I in 1992, and third gear acceleration came out better than the Ferrari Testarossa of the period.

Maintenance

Engine oil level should be checked when parked, engine off, and dipped twice and wiped from level on dipstick, then run the car for two minutes, and check again, engine oil level should be on max or not below max. Use recommended oils for top up, never use inferior or cheap oil.

I recommend you fill up your car in a recognised branded fuel station, not a supermarket for instance, and use 95RON minimum, 97RON up gives a tad of extra performance, and the car feels like it is running better, this is more expensive, however.

Cambelt and drive belts and tensioners should be changed every 20-25,000 miles or every three years, don't be tempted to skimp on the belts are doing a very important job. If you do this the engine will last much longer and higher mileage is achievable. If the engine is not smooth it could be down to balancer shaft belts needing attention or being tensioned incorrectly.

Brakes need to be working well, so have a quick look at the pads and disc for scoring. A service should take care of your fluids, filters and lubrication of necessary parts, worn wheel bearings can make a noise on take up of speed and decreasing of wheel rotation. It's a good idea to check transmission oil levels when the car is being serviced. Door locks and catches should be oiled with a lubricating spray, for longer life and ease of use.

General maintenance

Always check the rear tailgate channel where it meets the roof as water, leaves etc can sit there and rot, this channel should be kept clean and dry. I recommend washing the car by hand with a few buckets and different sponges for top/middle/bottom of bodywork to minimise scratching, dried off with a leather, it is not a good idea to garage the car when wet. Use of shampoo is kept to a minimum as it fades paint and you will have to polish.

Cars fitted with A/C need the A/C serviced bi-annually as they can leak and therefore efficiency is reduced; it may need a re-gas. Please remember that the system is not a modern one, and there is an awful lot of heat being generated under the bonnet, it works well if working to optimum capability. Check under front footwell carpets periodically for evidence of leaking A/C fluids sitting underneath, which causes rot.

Summary

You have opted to buy a Lancia Delta integrale, and it's almost a certainty that you know what you are getting: an exceptionally high-performance car based on an '80s hatchback. You will know it has Italian heritage. For this you will sacrifice a little comfort and a fair amount of money over a normal hatchback, but you will get one of the universally acknowledged best homologation specials, with probably the best road manners of its type, along with the many foibles (or character) of an Italian car.

They come only in left-hand drive. They can be converted, but conversions are less valuable, not as good, and lose most of the superbly developed handling attributes. Properly serviced they are reasonably durable. As six times World Rally

Champion, its value will always be recognised and highly sought after. As always, buyer beware: any lack of servicing or variation from standard could land you in very deep water.

Have a budget to adhere to before you go to view a car. A cheap car is probably cheap for a good reason, and a poorly maintained car can cost a large amount to rectify, so if you do the checks, you should have a better idea of likely spending post purchase. Always get the best car you can for your budget. Check the service history and what has been done, knowing this can help you factor in what may need attention after purchase, corresponding with bills, stamps and service schedules.

The integrale was only ever made in left-hand drive – although this example has been converted to right-hand drive. Conversions may lose some of their handling attributes, and will always be less valuable due to lack of originality. This Lord Blue Evo II was converted to RHD by John Whalley Ltd. (Courtesy Peter Collins)

4 Relative values
– which model for you?

It is no secret that the values of these sought-after cars have increased since they first came to market. There are prices being asked and paid that in my opinion are not always justified. The differences between some of the limited editions and standard cars are only exterior colour and interior trim, and yet some cars are priced at double or even triple the cost of a standard car. Of course a limited edition should command a premium, but not such a massive difference. A good example remains a solid purchase that should increase in value.

Of late, values have increased rapidly on some models such as Evo II limited editions, and overall for all models compared to just a few years ago. If you buy the right car, and buy the best you can get for your budget, you should do well, but remember to factor in the cost of any repairs, maintenance, or rectifying work. Be aware of originality and possible modifications, which will affect the value.

My advice is always go for as close to standard as possible – how it left the factory, that way your investment will command a higher value. A modified car is worth less, and may only appeal to buyers who want to use it in mild competition, want more performance, or to personalise it to their taste – a route which will ultimately devalue a car. The current trend of placing the limited editions at such a high value, compared to a standard coloured and trimmed version, is probably down to the limited number of cars produced. Generally, it is only the trim and exterior colour that are different. The Club Italia, for example, is always going to be more collectable, due to the car being personalised by the original owner, and only 15 were ever produced; however, the cars are the same underneath in all other editions.

The Evo II is regarded as the best model, it is more relaxed to drive, and it was mostly hand built, which made the assembly line move slowly. The cars were painted by Bertone, and then went to Chivasso for assembly – only five cars per day were made. Carrozzeria Maggiora, which built the cars, employed women on quality control as they were deemed to have a better eye for this kind of work.

Quality control at end of production, Chivasso 1994. Maggiora used female workers to perform the final checks, as they were deemed to have a better eye for detail.

Relative values

Relative values of different models are approximated below as percentages of the base models 16v or HF integrale. Check the current market value of base models in up-to-date magazines (although in my experience these are not always accurate), ask a specialist dealer, or look at recent auction prices.

HF 4WD	57% on average
8v integrale	70% on average
16v integrale	100%
HF integrale (Evo I or Deltona)	100% on average
HF integrale Evo II Cat (Deltona)	100% on average
Competition prepared	–30% on average
Concours	+20%
Special editions	+50% or more depending on edition.
Rally with works heritage	up to six times the value

Specification variants
Standard colours/trims

HF 4WD: Rosso Monza, White , Black metallic, Quartz Grey metallic, Turquoise metallic, Rosso Bordeaux metallic.

Cars as standard had Harlem striped interior, with standard seats (not Recaro) unless a cost option was available, then same material but Recaro seats in front.

8v integrale: Rosso Monza, White, Black metallic, Quartz Grey metallic, Rosso Bordeaux metallic. All but Rosso Monza are rare colours in this model. Standard Recaro seats were fitted with Harlem striping.

16v integrale: Rosso Monza, White, Black metallic, Quartz Grey metallic, Rosso Bordeaux metallic.

Interior trim featuring Harlem striping, as found in the 8v and 16v integrale.

Evo I/integrale 16v optional leather seats (also used in Gialla Ferrari edition).

In later production of this model, the Evo style interior was fitted to cars after late 1990, and in either Grey perforated Alcantara in red cars, and sometimes peppermint green in white or black cars.

Cars that were ordered as cost option of A/C and leather were always fitted with black perforated Recaro seats.

Evo I: Rosso Monza, White, Black metallic, Rosso Winner metallic, Derby Green metallic, Blue Madras metallic, Blue Lord. Blue Madras and Derby Green are very rare colours, and white is not common.

Interiors were either grey or green perforated Alcantara, or black leather.

Evo II: Rosso Monza, White, Blue Lord.

Standard interior was beige high back Recaro seats.

From the production numbers for other variants, the following number of limited editions were produced.

Club Italia: 1992 Evo I (15, with no number 13 for superstitious reasons). This series was produced for members of the exclusive Club Italia in Italy, who were Ferrari owners. Lancia was approached to make a small number of cars which were exclusive, each owner could pick their own personal specification with adjustable boost power upgrade for example. The cars had ERG fuel stickers applied to the rear wings near the fuel cap, and 'Club Italia' script on the rear spoiler and front bumper. Some owners wanted less script, so it was not applied, one car was made with hand controls for Clay Reggazzoni. The cars were painted Lord Blue, with dark red leather interior, had a Teflon bushing added to the gear selection, with carbon look surround, round ball on lever, drilled pedals, and push button ignition switch. There was a

Club Italia edition (below), and the Club Italia centre console plaque (inset). (Courtesy Peter Collins)

Club Italia edition. (Courtesy Peter Collins)

Club Italia Shield on top of the front wing, and an additional under bonnet edition numbered plate.

Hi Fi Club: Evo I (25) 18 blue, 7 red.
This series of cars produced in either Lord Blue or Rosso Monza, with the Torinese two yellow stripes with a light blue one in the centre, running across the roof and over the bonnet. They had different design Recaro seats trimmed in leather, matching door cards, special badging to front grille and bespoke leather luggage. The Hi Fi Club was for Lancia owners who had bought five new Lancias consecutively, and this enabled membership.

Lancia Club: Evo I (8) 4 blue, 4 red.
This edition was the same as the Hi Fi edition, but with an older style Lancia badge on the front wing made in porcelain.

Martini 5: (400) 1992.
Produced to celebrate the fifth world championship win in 1991. Painted white with Martini stripes, white wheels, black bonnet vents, black rear spoiler with 'Martini Racing' script. Red seatbelts, black Alcantara high back Recaro interior with red stitching, matching door cards, Solextra glass and Gemini Alarm system, Clarion Radio cassette. There was a number 5 on the left-hand tailgate badge to celebrate the world championship rally wins.

Martini 6: (310) 1992 (300 sold in Italy, 10 in Europe).
Made in late 1992, to celebrate the sixth world championship rally win. Painted white with Martini stripes (different to Martini 5), white wheels, 'Martini Racing' script on rear spoiler, Lancia Shield in middle of roof, 'World Rally Champion' script along bottom of doors, and front bumper HF stickers on the C-Pillars. Push button ignition, 16v steering wheel. Turquoise Alcantara high back Recaro seats with red

A Martini 5 at Chivasso LMC in 1994.

The Martini 6 edition. Note the 16v
steering wheel on the interior shot.
(Courtesy Peter Collins)

World Rally Champion limited edition. (Courtesy Peter Collins)

stitching, matching door cards, round gearlever top, Teflon bushes and carbon look plate. The glass was 'Solextra' in blue tint, and was fitted originally with Gemini Alarm system and Clarion radio/cassette. For the Martini 6 there was a number 6 on the left-hand tailgate badge to celebrate the world championship rally wins.

World Rally Champion: (580) 1992. 470 were produced with the 16v engine, and went to Italy (360), France (30), Belgium (40), Spain (20), and Portugal (20); there were also 180 Swiss spec 8v engine examples. Cars were finished in York Green, with tan leather Recaro high back seats. Special Tailgate badge on left side.

Gialla Ferrari: (295) October 1992, 245 for Italy, 50 for Germany.
A limited run was produced with black perforated Evo I seats and door cards.
    The edition was born due to two Juventus footballers who were under contract to arrive at home games in a Lancia, but wanted to be different. Gialla Ferrari was a particular colour with a link to Modena, so when these were produced, the marketing team decided to make this a limited run car.

Blue Lagos: (205) March-April 1994, 200 for Italy, 5 for Greece.
Cars were produced by Maggiora with magnolia leather high back Recaro seats, interior and door cards, yellow striping on the sides of the body. Two cars were delivered to the UK with standard beige Alcantara interior; they had been special order cars, ordered by Cloverleaf cars in Hampshire after the amount of leather had been produced for the run in Italy, therefore standard interior was fitted.

White Pearl: (370) 1994.
Interesting colour which changes in different lights: it looks white one moment, then appears to be silver. Grey stripes on body, blue leather high back Recaro seats, door cards and steering wheel.

Blue Lagos limited edition, and interior.

White Pearl limited edition, with interior (inset).
(Courtesy Peter Collins)

Dealers Collection limited edition, and interior.

Dealers Collection: (180) 1994/95.
Edition made to sell at traditionally successful integrale specialists in Italy, finished in Candy Red Metallic with tan leather high back Recaro seats, matching door cards, passenger rally foot rest, silver push button ignition, white instrument surround.

Gialla Ginestra: (220) 1994, 150 for Italy, 50 for Germany, 20 for France. Painted a different shade of yellow, with black high back Recaro Alcantara seats with yellow stitching, and matching door cards. Some cars were eventually supplied new by UK specialists.

Above: Gialla Ginestra limited editions at an LMC meet in 1995. (Courtesy Peter Collins)
Left and below, the Gialla Ginestra at Chivasso in 1994.

Japanese final edition, above: as shown in the promotional brochure, and left: the interior.

Japanese final edition:
(250) 1994/95.
Japanese importers of
Lancia approached the
company to make a special edition for their market. This edition has more special
features than any other, and generally commands a higher price for this. Painted
in Candy Red non-metallic, with black bonnet vents, Torinese striping along the
roof and bonnet, different tailgate badge on left side, Japanese indicator repeaters
on wings, Japanese spec headlights, carbon look gearlever surround and steering
wheel boss, ball type gearlever top, different boot at base of lever, drilled pedals,
push button ignition switch, white instrument surround, rear strut brace, dark grey
Alcantara high back Recaro seats with black cloth centres. The suspension used
Eibach 1in lower springs, wheels were silver on the edge and grey on the 'fan' part,
wire mesh grille with a number etched below the HF elephant badge, non-chrome
effect surround.

Colleczione: (22) 1994.
Made for French importers, run of just 22 cars in same spec as the 'World Rally Champion' in York Green with tan leather, but these were Evo II cars fitted with Cat.

Very limited editions
Viola Prototype: (1) 1994.
Finished in Viola Cardigan, this car was to be the new edition of Evo for 1995 model year and beyond, but only one exists as production was cancelled. It featured a viscous drive front differential, which increased grip, and road holding was improved. It had at least 250bhp, and a beige Alcantara interior.

Above and right:
The Viola Prototype,
at Chivasso 1995.
(Courtesy Peter
Collins)

Viola Prototype seen
during an LMC visit
in 1994, with visitors
being driven around
the factory test
track by Maggiora
test driver, Roberto
Franco.

Bronze metallic: (1) 1994. Produced for marketing department, fitted with beige Alcantara.

Pink metallic: (1) 1994. Pink metallic car with blue leather interior and steering wheel.

Silver metallic: (1) 1994. Was produced for a family member of Maggiora but was given to FIAT board member. Fitted with black Alcantara interior.

Cabriolet: (1) 1992.
Made exclusively for FIAT Chairman, Gianni Agnelli; produced by Reparto Pilotta, a special department within the FIAT experimental department. Heavily structured to eliminate scuttle shake, with elongated doors/glass installed. The car was fitted with electronic clutch originally, which has been converted to traditional lever/clutch today. The interior was a particular leather in anthracite which was used by the Agnelli family with matching door cards. The family had several integrale over the years with the same interior choice, and always in Silver Grey metallic exterior colour.

Pink metallic – a one-off colour, seen inside the Chivasso factory, 1994.

Silver metallic version, a one-off made for the Maggiora Director. Inside Chivasso, 1994. (Courtesy Peter Collins)

White Pearl Turin show car: (1) 1994.
This car was made for display at the Turin show in 1994. It was a different mica paint and looked more white than the other limited edition produced, had white door handles, and a complete beige Alcantara interior covering also the centre tunnel, dashboard.

Grey metallic: Agnelli Family. It is not known how many of this model was made for the Agnelli family, but at least one is still in use today, a special Silver Grey metallic exterior with dark blue/black high quality leather seats and door cards, other spec of these cars is not known.

The White Pearl show car at Chivasso, 1994. It was a one-off example, displayed at the Torino show. The colour was slightly different to the limited edition version, note colour coded door handles, and the dashboard and centre console covered with Alcantara to match the seats.
(Courtesy Peter Collins)

Silver Grey Agnelli family edition, unique version made for the family, and fitted with special quality leather interior and door cards.

5 Before you view
– be well informed

To avoid a wasted journey, and the disappointment of finding that the car does not match your expectations, it will help if you're very clear about what questions you want to ask before you pick up the telephone. Some of these points might appear basic but when you're excited about the prospect of buying your dream classic, it's amazing how some of the most obvious things slip the mind. Also check the current values of the model you are interested in, some classic car magazines do not have up-to-date accurate values but may give auction results.

Where is the car?
Is it going to be worth travelling to the next county/ state, or even across a border? A locally advertised car, although it may not sound very interesting, can add to your knowledge for very little effort, so make a visit – it might even be in better condition than expected.

Dealer or private sale?
Establish early on if the car is being sold by its owner or by a trader. A private owner should have all the history, so don't be afraid to ask detailed questions. A dealer may have more limited knowledge of a car's history, but should have some documentation. A dealer may offer a warranty/guarantee (ask for a printed copy) and finance.

Cost of collection and delivery?
A dealer may well be used to quoting for delivery by car transporter. A private owner may agree to meet you halfway, but only agree to this after you have seen the car at the vendor's address to validate the documents. Conversely, you could meet halfway and agree the sale, but insist on meeting at the vendor's address for the handover.

View – when and where?
It is always preferable to view at the vendor's home or business premises. In the case of a private sale, the car's documentation should tally with the vendor's name and address. Arrange to view only in daylight and avoid a wet day. Most cars look better in poor light or when wet.

Reason for sale?
Do make it one of the first questions. Why is the car being sold and how long has it been with the current owner? How many previous owners?

Imports
If a steering conversion has been done it can only reduce the value. When you buy a car from another country, you may need to make changes to the number (licence) plates, lighting (headlamps and indicators) and radio equipment. If you re-register a car from Germany or elsewhere in the EU in another country, you may need to obtain a certificate of conformity from FCA that it conforms to the original specification.

Condition (body/chassis/interior/mechanicals)?
Ask for an honest appraisal of the car's condition. Ask specifically about some of the check items described in chapter 7.

All original specification
An original equipment car is invariably of higher value than a customised/modified version.

It is essential that you check the documents for the car you are thinking of buying in various ways, for example the MOT history, verifying the mileage, checking the details of the keeper and the person selling the car. On foreign cars, checking the registration documents carefully, making sure it is an official document, checking the details within, is there proof of duty paid from a non-EU country?

Doing a HPI check is also a good idea.

Matching data/legal ownership
Do VIN/chassis, engine numbers and licence plate match the official registration document? Is the owner's name and address recorded in the official registration documents?

For those countries that require an annual test of roadworthiness, does the car have a document showing it complies (an MOT certificate in the UK, which can be verified on 0300 123 9000 or online at gov.uk/check-mot-status)?

If a smog/emissions certificate is mandatory, does the car have one?

If required, does the car carry a current road fund license/licence plate tag?

Does the vendor own the car outright? Money might be owed to a finance company or bank: the car could even be stolen. Several organisations will supply the data on ownership, based on the car's licence plate number, for a fee. Such companies can often also tel you whether the car has been 'written-off' by an insurance company. In the UK these organisations can supply vehicle data:

DVLA	0844 453 0118
HPI	0113 222 2010
AA	0800 056 8040
RAC	0330 159 0364

Other countries will have similar organisations.

Insurance
Check with your existing insurer before setting out, your current policy might not cover you to drive the car if you do purchase it.

How you can pay?
A cheque/check will take several days to clear and the seller may prefer to sell to a cash buyer. However, a banker's draft (a cheque issued by a bank) is a good as cash, but safer, so contact your own bank and become familiar with the formalities that are necessary to obtain one. Bank transfer is another possibility, and is a convenient option if you use internet banking.

Buying at auction?
If the intention is to buy at auction see chapter 10 for further advice.

Professional vehicle check (mechanical examination)

There are often marque/model specialists who will undertake professional examination of a vehicle on your behalf. Owners' clubs will be able to put you in touch with such specialists.

Other organisations that will carry out a general professional check in the UK:

AA: 0800 056 8040 / www.theaa.com/vehicle-inspection (motoring organisation with vehicle inspectors)
RAC: 0330 159 0720 / www.rac.co.uk/buying-a-car/vehicle-inspections (motoring organisation with vehicle inspectors)

Other countries will have similar organisations.

6 Inspection equipment
– these items will really help

- This book
- Reading glasses (if you need them for close work)
- Magnet (not powerful, a fridge magnet is ideal)
- Torch
- Probe (a small screwdriver works very well)
- Overalls
- Mirror on a stick
- Digital camera
- A friend, preferably a knowledgeable enthusiast

Before you rush out of the door, gather together a few items that will help as you work your way around the car. This book is designed to be your guide at every step, so take it along and use the check boxes to help you assess each area of the car you're interested in. Don't be afraid to let the seller see you using it.

Take your reading glasses if you need them to read documents and make close up inspections.

A magnet will help you check if the car is full of filler, or has fibreglass panels. Use the magnet to sample bodywork areas all around the car, but be careful not to damage the paintwork. Expect to find a little filler here and there, but not whole panels. There's nothing wrong with fibreglass panels, but a purist might want the car to be as original as possible.

A torch with fresh batteries will be useful for peering into the wheelarches and under the car.

A small screwdriver can be used – with care – as a probe, particularly in the wheelarches and on the underside. With this you should be able to check an area of severe corrosion, but be careful – if it's really bad the screwdriver might go right through the metal!

Be prepared to get dirty. Take along a pair of overalls, if you have them. Fixing a mirror at an angle on the end of a stick may seem odd, but you'll probably need it to check the condition of the underside of the car. It will also help you to peer into some of the important crevices. You can also use it, together with the torch, along the underside of the sills and on the floor.

If you have the use of a digital camera, take it along so that later you can study some areas of the car more closely. Take a picture of any part of the car that causes you concern, and seek a friend's opinion.

Ideally, have a friend or knowledgeable enthusiast accompany you: a second opinion is always valuable.

Standard White Pearl Limited Edition, Italian import circa 1998.
(Courtesy Peter Collins)

7 Fifteen minute evaluation

– walk away or stay?

The integrale was a sophisticated car when new, but with relatively few good cars on the market, it is more important than ever to assess each example with care. There is some chance the car was once used for rallying or competition work.

Start your 15 minute evaluation with a two-metre walk around: stand two metres from the car and study it. Check that its body sits level and square on the road. Look at each wheel relative to the body and wheelarch line. Are all four consistent? Do they match, does one tyre seem to stick out more than another? Do they all point in the same direction? No? Walk away.

Next, look closely at the external bodywork and features. Look for signs of rally work, accident damage, poorly executed or damaged paintwork, poor lustre, stone chips, and overall wear and tear to the bodywork. The car is likely to get stone chips on the bonnet, the lower part of the doors, A pillars, windscreen or the door, though these can be minimised by fitting front mudflaps. Open and close the doors to assess the fit. Panel gaps were not to Japanese standards, but gaps ought to be consistent and flush with the next panel.

Use touch on all the panels and gaps, you will notice if there are badly fitting panels or differences in paint quality.

Check inside wheelarches and liners if possible.

Is the interior tidy or tatty? Can you see or smell oil, fuel, brake fluid or indeed anything else that indicates that it hasn't been cared for? Do the carpets look like they have all been out at some stage?

Look for stray loose nuts, bolts, fittings or broken bits in the centre console or glove box. If you find any, chances are you are looking at a rebuilt car, and not very well at that.

Do any warning lights come on when the engine is running? Did it start easily? Does it smoke on start-up or when revved?

Do the boot carpets look like they have always been there?

The engine compartment need not be spotless, but check belt tension on the ones you can see. Look and smell for serious leaks, and listen for strange noises. Look at the inner wings and under bonnet panels for signs someone has been there with a hammer or a clamp.

Chassis numbers are found on earlier cars up to Evo, stamped on the suspension turret, with the chassis plate fixed below. (See chapter 9 for examples of chassis plates.)

Evo I and 2 models have a stamp on the inner wing under the A/C piping on the passenger side, and corresponding chassis plate is located next to the spares number on the front splash panel to which the bonnet is hinged. Check that the numbers don't look tampered with, or even ground away entirely. Check the rivets have not been tampered with.

If happy with the checks so far, you can proceed to the 60 minute evaluation in chapter 9. If not, ask further questions and recheck items of concern, these could be bargaining points – or walk away.

8 Key points
– where to look for problems

Numbers
- Does the VIN code match the chassis and body number stamps, do they and the engine number match the registration document?
- Do the documents show when it was imported and where from?
- Does the VIN code match the specification?
- Do the mileage tumblers line up, does the mileage seem likely, given the condition?
- Is there a service history with the car?
- Are there bills and invoices that show regular maintenance.

Exterior
- Are all the panels straight, with even gaps?
- Are there signs of corrosion, particularly on the wings, doors and sills and around the sunroof (if fitted) and tailgate. Is the paint a lustrous, consistent finish and the same colour all over?
- Are the seals for the doors and windows in good order?
- Check tailgate apertures. Any stress cracks on the floor or inside the front door apertures under the felt trim on A Pillars?

Interior
- Does the overall condition of the interior appear consistent with the mileage shown?
- Can you see or smell any signs of fuel, oil or damp under the carpets or stains on the headlining (especially if a sunroof is fitted)?
- Is the Alcantara or leather upholstery in good condition, or is it cracked faded and worn?
- Is any of the plastic trim cracked or missing?
- Do the top of door cards fit well and straight? Check for signs of wear on steering wheel, gearlever and pedals.
- If air-conditioning is fitted, does this still work properly?

Engine and mechanical
- Does the engine compartment appear clean, without any major oil or coolant leaks?
- Are the hoses and wires secure and in good condition?
- Check hoses and air filter are standard
- Does the engine start run smoothly, without blue or black smoke from the exhaust?
- If you can look underneath, are the chassis and suspension free from rust?
- Is there a service history with the car?
- Is the coolant completely blue with no signs of oil?
- Is the dipstick clean showing good oil level?
- Evo IIs have a later one small coil per bank ignition system, earlier cars had traditional distributor/coil setup.

If you've come this far, well done! The paperwork is in order and the car looks promising. Now is the time to take a really thorough look over it, bearing in mind the points already mentioned in the last two chapters. Try and work your way systematically around the car, so that you don't miss any details. Start outside with a close look at the bodywork, before turning your attention to the interior and finally the engine and underbody.

Score each section using the boxes as follows:
4 = excellent; 3 = good; 2 = average; 1 = poor. The totting-up procedure is detailed at the end of the chapter. Be realistic in your marking!

Exterior
Bodywork

Check A pillars for chips, also pull back the felt material on the upper edge of the door aperture, and check for stress cracks.

Peel back the windscreen rubber seals and look behind for possible corrosion; check the front scuttle beside the wipers too.

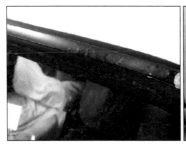 

Check around windscreen rubbers for corrosion and the A pillars for stone chips.

HF 4WD striping as standard.

Check if the car has modifications applied to it? For example, a rear spoiler fitted that is not original, or later rain gutters fitted to an earlier car. (Earlier integrales up to and including Evo I had the same roof gutters, only Evo IIs had wider flatter type).

Check for original colours and badging: bonnet louvres are generally colour coded except for some limited editions (Martini 5) Evo I, or HF 4WD where they are black. HF 4WD, 8v integrale and 16v integrale have matt black sills that are not colour coded, and the original grille surround should be stainless steel and not painted. HF 4WD had two side stripes as standard, one at the base of the door glass, and the usual coachline.

Badging is particular to each model, and this should be retained. UK Evo IIs were badged Montecarlo on the left of the tailgate. German cars were badged Sedici on the front doors, halfway up at the leading edge. All limited edition cars had particular badges relating to the edition, with the exception of the Dealers Collection, Blue Lagos and White Pearl.

Open and close the doors. Do they close easily? Check panel gaps are uniform, check panel gaps on tailgate: they should be the same on both sides.

Integrale matt black sill as standard.

Corrosion

Look all around the screen area and under the bonnet for evidence of corrosion, and check all bodywork for corrosion caused by accident damage. Look around the inside of the wheelarches for corrosion or mud build up. Check channel on the open tailgate where it meets the roof. If a sunroof is fitted, check the channel around it for corrosion.

Tailgate badges – from the top: Martini 6; Sedici German market limited edition badge; World Rally Champion. (Courtesy Peter Collins)

Chassis and sills

Check jacking points for damage

Tailgate channel and rear window rubber seal to be checked for corrosion.

The jacking point: this is what can happen if car was incorrectly jacked up.

Front offside – another area to check for possible corrosion.

Check around the sunroof for corrosion.

Seat anchorage point: check underside, as it can crack the floor.

caused by incorrect jacking in the past. Check the rear subframe, front subframe, subframe to inner wing, and the seatbelt anchorage points which can crack the floor. Take a good look at side skirts on side of vehicle to look for signs of corrosion underneath. A wheelarch liner being taken out is the only way to check correctly if the wheelarches have corrosion. Check underneath carpets for excess evidence of water leak from air-conditioning or heater to the floor and base of the windscreen having leaked in the past.

Underbody

Check the rear floor in the area of the rear differential and carrier, where it is supported and attaches to the body. Check the exhaust brackets and the catalytic converter (Evo II).

Glass

Check if the windscreen and glass are original. Each model had a different tint, from green to bronze and blue. Check for a Lancia shield on the windscreen and on other glass, the codes should match on the etched script.

Wheels and tyres

Tyres should have the same tread pattern on each axle, and be even in wear. The handling is better on a tyre with a stiff shoulder as you can have more confidence in turn in; a softer shoulder feels like you are losing grip. Goodyear makes a suitable tyre for the earlier models, Bridgestone is another good brand, and Michelin tyres are very good for wear, but are made of a hard compound, Pirelli P Zero is the best tyre for Evo models (and I believe they are being remanufactured), although not the Nero version, as the shoulder is too soft. I also hear good things about Hankook, and Yokohama if you like grip over longevity. I think everyone has their own preferred brand at the end of the day. Price and availability is also a factor.

Wheel types, top left: HF 4WD standard road wheel; bottom left: integrale 8v standard roadwheel (note 8v is not dished as much as 16v, but is the same design); top right integrale 16v standard roadwheel; bottom right: Evo standard roadwheel, 15in on Evo I, 16in on Evo II. (HF 4WD photograph courtesy Peter Collins)

Check if wheels are standard or aftermarket. Standard wheels are always best.

The 4WD had a similar wheel design to the HF Turbo, the 8v & 16v integrale had the same design, albeit enlarged and slightly dished for 16v; the Evo I had 15in wheels, Evo II had 16in wheels.

On Evo models, there is a road wheel available in 17in, the same design as standard wheels but larger, called the Speedline Montecarlo. This is aesthetically pleasing as it fills the wheelarch, but it is not homologated for road use, and can crack.

Check for any uneven tyre wear and flat spots on tyres.

Interior
Seats and upholstery

Are the seats standard or aftermarket? If standard, check seat bolsters for sagging and heavy creasing, seat material for snagging, cracking (leather); operation of the extendible under-knee extension (HF 4WD, 8v, 16v and Evo I), and overall operation of seats.

The seats in the HF 4WD were covered in grey Alcantara and had the 'Harlem'

Standard HF 4WD seats, in grey Alcantara with 'Harlem'-patterned cloth in the centre. (Courtesy Peter Collins)

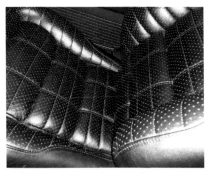

Leather seat as seen in Evo I and 2 limited editions.

Standard integrale seats, Recaro with knee support, option on HF 4WD.

Standard Evo I perforated Alcantara seats, in grey or green.

Standard Evo II seats – beige Alcantara high back Recaros with HF in headrest.

striped pattern on cloth in the centre (manufactured by Missoni): they were not Recaro design unless you paid for them as a cost option; in that case they were the same as the later 8v and 16v integrale seat design by Recaro. The material is washable, but cloth can snag, bolsters may wear with hard use, and the material can 'pile' with wear.

A cost option for 16v and Evo I was black perforated leather, which came with A/C as a package. The Evo I and 2 limited editions generally had leather interior as standard, with the exception of Martini 5 and 6 editions.

Interior trim

Some describe the interior dashboard and trim as gimcrack, which is a little harsh: it is generally okay, there may be some squeaks and rattles that can generally be overcome ... once you have located the noise.

Look for signs in the floor and the upholstery that a roll cage has been fitted, as this could be a strong negotiating point.

Check the roof lining for sagging, though this can be rectified and is not a major issue.

What is the condition of the door cards? Do they fit the door properly without a large gap at the top? Is the carpet in good order? If possible, look under the carpet for legacy leaks onto the floor or pedal area. Does the car smell of petrol inside? This can be caused by a poor union to the fuel pump under the floor in the rear of the cabin. Are the seatbelts original? Cars used on track days and/or modified may have been fitted with a harness. Check anchorage points.

Is the centre tunnel marked and scratched? Are there any cracks in the dashboard? Check operation of the glovebox and key. Wear on the gearlever or on the steering wheel indicates high use. Check pedal rubbers for wear. Is the gearlever standard type? HF 4WD, 8v and 16v gearlevers should look like the photo on the right.

Is the steering wheel standard type? Aftermarket steering wheels never add value. Standard steering wheels for 8v, 16v and Martini 6 Evo I, Evo I and Evo II Cat are shown on the next page.

The integrale and HF 4WD standard gearlever. Note, Evo versions had a more ergonomic top with a section for your thumb to grip; there's no reason to modify this!

45

Left: integrale and HF 4WD standard steering wheel, also used on Martini 6 limited edition.
Top right: standard Evo I steering wheel.
Bottom right: Standard Evo II Momo corse steering wheel.

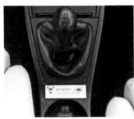

Limited edition models had a limited edition plaque on the centre tunnel, just in front of the handbrake below the gearlever, some were stamped, some not, usually with either a number or original owner's name, which was put on by themselves, not the factory.

Limited edition plaque, attached to centre console below gearlever. (Courtesy Peter Collins)

Boot/trunk

Check the load area inside the tailgate, on the left side is a small door which, when opened, contains the rear window washer reservoir, check this is not cracked and leaking as this leads to water running into the load area floor, and the underside of the car can corrode. On the right there is a small round bulb which, when twisted, gives light to this area, but this only operates when the lights are switched on, so it's a good idea to have the engine running so as not to discharge the battery.

In this area is the space saver spare wheel, which is hardly ever used, so should be in very good condition. It should be inflated to the correct pressure and be fixed into the body by a bolt; these sit in a black vinyl cover also containing the tool kit, comprising a jack, screwdriver and handle.

If using the spare wheel, do not exceed the speed advised, it is only intended to get you home or the tyre shop.

For homologation purposes some cars might have a water spray system fitted with spray nozzles in the area of the intercooler, with a bag in the boot next to the water reservoir. This system is not connected and will not work. This does not make this car special; but a certain number of cars had to have this equipment in order to homologate the rally car.

Electrics

General electrical check

Check if the electric windows are working okay, along with the windscreen washers, rear wiper and headlights. Is the handbrake working okay without being too high? Check the operation of heater fan, heater and/or A/C.

Air con and heating

A/C-fitted cars can leak gas, so check that the car gets fully cold on max and stays there, with no damp smell; if it doesn't get/stay cold it probably means a re-gas is necessary. Only the 16v, Evos 1 and 2 had air-conditioning fitted (16v and Evo I was a cost option) and this works but not to today's standards. An A/C check every now and then optimises the functionality.

The heating system works well, but ventilation is not to modern standards. You may need the window opened a little in driving rain, for example. The heater system is controlled by three circular controls, one for temperature, one for fan speed, and the other for direction of air.

Instruments and controls

The switchgear is somewhat dated but works well, located on thin spindles, with the indicators on the left side, and another for lights which you turn at the end, and use for full beam. Use the right-hand side for wipers and washers.

A button in the centre console operates the rear wiper, which is either constantly on or off, with no intermittent wipe, which can be slightly annoying at times. There is also an array of buttons for hazard warning, fog lights, and so on. The gauges on the dash are easily readable, and give all the information you need about the battery charge, fuel, coolant temperature, boost gauge, and, in the centre, oil temperature and pressure. My advice is get fuel as soon as it gets low, do

The check panel which monitors vehicle condition, oil level, bulbs, etc. The check panal was not fitted as standard to UK cars, they were fitted with an electric sunroof and a cubby hole instead.

not wait until the orange light comes on, as over time the sender unit may be worn and give a false reading.

For cars fitted with a sunroof, the small cubby hole in the dash may have been filled with a switch for an electric motor (UK spec), some cars had manual opening (European spec), and this also meant there was no car condition check panel. On cars fitted with this panel, the driver is alerted to possible faults with sensors, door openings, light bulb failure, and, in some cases, this can show misleading faults which is usually due to a faulty earth. The clock is digital and is above the top of the windscreen. Front window switches are in the centre tunnel beside the handbrake lever, the headlamp adjustment is also found here.

Check all the instruments work when the ignition is switched on and they indicate a realistic reading, are there any warning lights on? The car is getting to the age where indicator stalks and other switches and handles start to give up, so check them all carefully.

Lights
Check all the lights operate correctly. Make sure they work at the right time, point in the right direction, and lenses are unbroken.

Audio system
Is the audio system standard or aftermarket? Check there are no holes in the trim for massive speakers, and that speakers do not have interference. Check the original parcel shelf is evident, as it is sometimes substituted with an acoustic type for installation of speakers.

Engine and mechanical
Gearbox/ differentials
Although complex, the transmission does not present problems if maintained well. When driving the car you will hear a very slight differential noise, but not a loud whine; if this is present, it will need investigating, as there are three differentials; one at the front, one at the rear, and a centre Torsen differential. Each one of these costs upward of £1800 to replace, and parts are not easy to get. A recondition will also cost a reasonable amount, the take up of transmission can sometimes make a small clonk in reverse but this is nothing to worry about, a clonking going forward on clutch take up is more of a concern. Gear selection should be smooth, should not baulk, and has a shortish throw. The clutch is progressive and hydraulic on later models, so this should also work smoothly.

As there are three differentials they will make a degree of mechanical noise, but they should not whine or change when the load is increased or decreased. They should also not be leaking excessive oil and have the correct oil level. Gear selection should be straightforward, not too slack, and on take up of the clutch the car should move without excessive transmission making a clonking sound.

Exhaust
Standard systems are fine, they make a good enough sound, but there are some tailored systems you may want to use which enhance the sound of the car, which can increase the performance by a few bhp. Stainless material is recommended as moisture tends to rot the mild steel from inside out, especially if the car is not used much. Is the exhaust system standard? Is it too loud? Does

Integrale 8v and 16v standard exhausts always have twin pipes.

this mean it is a sports system? Has the catalyser been removed? (Evo II). 8v and 16v models had twin exhaust pipes, anything else is an aftermarket system. Does it leak?

Suspension

The standard suspension is fine, and is robust. On poor road surfaces the car has a hard feel, which is ultimately forgivable, but evident. The suspension is multi adjustable, camber is easily adjusted, caster can also be done, but more complicated to do, as you may have to re-align and move dampers. The car should be set up and checked at the rear first, if it is done front first, it will not be correct. Individuals sometimes prefer their own setup for geometry – more negative camber on the front to increase turn in, for example, but I would recommend you stay with factory settings, and to get a 4WD specialist tracker to do this. Specialists who have been involved with these cars should be able to do this without issue, as they know the cars so well. There are non-standard springs which are shorter, hence an inch lower in ride height, which are not recommended as it increases stress on the bodyshell, and can crack in the front door apertures. The dampers should be working well and in unison, if not it can feel like one side is hard and the other soft when under load; this points to rebound/depress issues. Anti-roll bar bushes wear and need to be checked, and the rose joints on Evo models wear faster, but this is evident from a vibration under the driver's left foot – a constant knocking feeling. The suspension should not creak or knock, and should give adequate rebound and compression from struts and springs. If the suspension appears to be very hard it could mean that the shock absorber is not working properly.

Steering

On lock the steering wheel should move freely while on the move, and should show a slight degree of feedback without making excessive noise, or clonking or squealing. Wheel balancing can be a factor if you get a shake through the wheel from side to side above 50mph to 75mph. The wheel should read dead straight with the Lancia Shield on the wheel boss showing straight, a slight turn either way should start the car turning, and within about an inch you can feel it changing direction. The power steering system is excellent and gives great feel and balance, there should be no noise from the power steering – no screech, whoosh or clonking – and no

A standard Evo II engine bay with no modifications.

loss of fluid in the reservoir. There should be no feedback through the wheel; a slight shimmy and vibration between 50-70 is normally attributed to poor balancing of the wheels. Tyre pressures are important, I always use 2.0 BAR all round, 2.1/2.2 is usually recommended for Evo models, but I found it too hard. If the steering geometry is set incorrectly, the car can tramline, or crab – a good indication of this is uneven tyre wear.

Brakes

The cars brake very well, and should do so in a straight line, no scoring on discs, and pads need to be up to scratch (as mentioned before). Evo models sometimes squeal, which can be rectified but it always comes back. The brakes are more than adequate for road use, but for track use, you may want to upgrade to Brembo Gold calipers/pads, which reduce brake fade when you are standing on the middle pedal for longer than normal. You could also upgrade the fluid to a racing type. Discs and pads should be checked for condition, no score marks on the discs and they should run freely. Pad wear is good in normal driving conditions, but spirited driving and standing on the brake pedal hard to decrease speed will certainly shorten their life.

Engine

Check operation of the turbo (on starting the engine there should be no excessive smoke when cold, or excessive smoke under load), and also the intercooler and oil cooler pipework. Look for leaks etc: there shouldn't be excessive tappet noise, just a small degree of ticking. The cars make a distinctive whirring sound. Cold and hot starting are not usually an issue, and the car should idle evenly, if it does not and revs high and stays up it could be down to one of the electric potentiometer units failing.

Under the bonnet (hood)

Can you do a compression test? Check the oil level, is it clean and up to the maximum mark? What oil has been used? Are there any signs of head gasket issues (water in oil/oil in water), any obvious oil or coolant leaks? Does the car run up to temperature and does the cooling fan work? Are there any signs of repairs under the bonnet that haven't been cleaned up? Check the reservoirs are clean and full. Are hoses original? Are there any signs of modifications?

Check whether air cleaner/plug leads have been replaced with aftermarket items such as Samco. An Evo engine bay should look like the Evo II example pictured on the next page.

(93-95) Made at Chivasso plant under licence by Carrozzeria Maggiora SRL. The codes can be read from the chassis plate inside the engine bay.

HF 4WD, 8v, 16v integrale models have a plate attached to the passenger side suspension turret, if the plate is blue it is an Italian spec car, a red plate is UK spec, Black is German and yellow Spanish spec. Some cars have the later silver plate which is attached to the scuttle which were fitted to the later cars (Evos).

Left: integrale suspension turret chassis plate.
Above: an Evo chassis plate on the splash panel.

Road test

Does the engine start easily? Is there any smoke from the exhaust? How does the engine sound, there should be no clonking or loud tapping. Does the clutch work well? Is gear engagement simple? There should be no baulking, or slippage? Does the clutch work well? Listen out for gearbox whine or differential noise. Does the car steer immediately side to side, with no noise or graunch from the steering rack? Power steering should work well with no noise. Listen for wheel bearing noise. Does the car track straight? Are there any suspension clonks or a slight clunking under the driver's left foot? Do the brakes pull up well and straight, with no noise (Evos excepted!)? Is the engine pulling cleanly, and the turbo working well on over boost? Does it idle smoothly? Check the gauges, is

Oil pressure and temperature gauges. Pressure should be over the second mark on the gauge when the engine is warm. On hard use temperature will rise from the centre. Both gauges should register in the centre on normal use.

The red warning light, under the rev counter; if any light appears on the check panel, this will illuminate, also it will not go out if the engine system has a fault.

The voltmeter shows the battery charge condition: a poor earth can make this fluctuate, giving an incorrect reading, and can also affect the fuel gauge.

coolant temperature at half point when warmed up, when fan is not working? If it increases, does the fan cut in?

Is the oil temperature under load at around half point? Is the oil pressure at halfway point? At idle it can drop to the second mark on gauge. The voltmeter fluctuates, it should read between 10-12 volts. If the car is fitted with a check panel indicator, are any lights showing? Check the red warning light on the dashboard (this shows if there is an injection system fault, and is also hooked up to various engine sensors); if it stays on two seconds after starting, there is a fault – the light should go out. Check operation of the warning lights and panels.

On the Evo models, the gauges are in the same place, but with different graphics.

The Evo instrument panel.

Evaluation procedure

Add up the total points from each section.

Score: 88 = excellent; 66 = good; 44 = average; 22 = poor.

Cars scoring between 22 and 43 will require some serious work (at much the same cost regardless of score).

Cars scoring between 44 and 65 will require very careful assessment of the necessary repair/restoration costs in order to arrive at a realistic value.

Cars scoring 66 or over will be completely usable and will require only maintenance and care to preserve condition.

10 Auctions
– sold! Another way to buy your dream

Auction pros & cons
Pros: Prices are often lower than those of dealers or private sellers and you might grab a real bargain on the day. Auctioneers have generally established clear title with the seller. At the venue you can usually examine documentation relating to the vehicle.

Cons: You have to rely on a sketchy catalogue description of condition and history. The opportunity to inspect is limited and you cannot drive the car. Auction cars are often a little below par and may require some work. It's easy to overbid. There will usually be a buyer's premium to pay in addition to the auction hammer price.

Which auction?
Auctions by established auctioneers are advertised in car magazines and on the auction houses' websites. A catalogue, or a simple printed list of the lots for auctions might only be available a day or two ahead, though often lots are listed and pictured on auctioneers' websites much earlier. Contact the auction company to ask if previous auction selling prices are available, as this is useful information (details of past sales are often available on websites).

When you purchase the catalogue of vehicles in an auction, it often acts as a ticket allowing two people to attend the viewing days and the auction. Catalogue details tend to be comparatively brief, but will include information such as 'one owner from new, low mileage, full service history,' etc. It will also usually show a guide price to give you some idea of what to expect to pay, and will tell you what is charged as a 'Buyer's premium.' The catalogue will also contain details of acceptable forms of payment. At the fall of the hammer an immediate deposit is usually required, the balance payable within 24 hours. If the plan is to pay by cash, there may be a cash limit. Some auctions will accept payment by debit card. Sometimes credit or charge cards are acceptable but will often incur an extra charge. A bank draft or bank transfer will have to be arranged in advance with your own bank as well as with the auction house. No car will be released before all payments are cleared. If delays occur in payment transfers, then storage costs can accrue.

A buyer's premium will be added to the hammer price: don't forget this in your calculations. It is not usual for there to be a further state tax or local tax on the purchase price and/or on the buyer's premium.

Viewing
In some instances, it's possible to view on the day or days before, as well as in the hours prior to the auction. There are usually auction officials available who are willing to help out by opening engine and luggage compartments and to allow you to inspect the interior.

While the officials may start the engine for you, a test drive is usually out of the question. Crawling under and around the car as much as you want is permitted, but you can't suggest that the car you are interested in be jacked up, or attempt to do the job yourself. You can also ask to see any documentation available.

Bidding

Before you take part in the auction, decide your maximum bid – and stick to it! It may take a while for the auctioneer to reach the lot you are interested in, so use that time to observe how other bidders behave. When it's the turn of your car, attract the auctioneer's attention and make an early bid. The auctioneer will then look to you for a reaction every time another bid is made, usually the bids will be in fixed increments until the bidding slows, when smaller increments will often be accepted before the hammer falls. If you want to withdraw from the bidding, make sure the auctioneer understands your intentions – a vigorous shake of the head when he or she looks to you for the next bid should do the trick! Assuming that you are the successful bidder, the auctioneer will note your card or paddle number, and from that moment on you will be responsible for the vehicle. If the car is unsold, either because it failed to reach the reserve or because there was little interest, it may be possible to negotiate with the owner, via the auctioneers, after the sale is over.

There are two more items to think about. How to get the car home, and insurance. If you can't drive the car, a trailer, your own or hired, is one way, another is to have the vehicle shipped using the facilities of a local company. The auction house will also have details of companies specialising in the transfer of cars.

Successful bid

Insurance for immediate cover can usually be purchased on site, but it may be more cost-effective to make arrangements with your own insurance company in advance, and then call to confirm the full details.

eBay and other online auctions

eBay and other online auctions could land you a car at a bargain price, though you'd be foolhardy to bid without examining the car first, something most vendors encourage. A useful feature of eBay is that the geographical location of the car is shown, so you can narrow your choices to those within a realistic radius of home. Be prepared to be outbid in the last few moments of the auction. Remember, your bid is binding and that it will be very, very difficult to get restitution in the case of a crooked vendor fleecing you – caveat emptor!

Be aware that some cars offered for sale in online auctions are 'ghost' cars. Don't part with any cash without being sure that the vehicle actually exists and is as described (usually pre-bidding inspection is possible).

Auctioneers

Barrett-Jackson www.barrett-jackson.com/ Bonhams www.bonhams.com/ Coys www.coys.co.uk/ eBay www.eBay.com/ H&H www.handh.co.uk/ RM Sotheby's www.rmsothebys.com/ Shannons www.shannons.com.au/ Silver www.silverauctions.com

11 Paperwork
– correct documentation is essential!

The paper trail

Enthusiasts' cars often come with a large portfolio of paperwork accumulated by a succession of proud owners. This documentation represents the real history of the car and shows the level of care the car has received, how it's been used, which specialists have worked on it and the dates of major repairs.

Registration documents

All countries/states have some form of registration for private vehicles, whether it's like the American 'pink slip' system or the British 'logbook' system.

It is essential to check that the registration document is genuine, that it relates to the car in question, and that all the vehicle's details are correctly recorded, including chassis/VIN (Vehicle Identification Number) and engine numbers (if these are shown). If you are buying from the previous owner, his or her name and address will be recorded in the document; this will not be the case if you are buying from a dealer.

In the UK, the current (Euro- aligned) registration document is named 'V5C,' and is printed in coloured sections. The blue section relates to the car specification, the green section has details of the new owner and the pink section is sent to the DVLA in the UK when the car is sold. A small section in yellow deals with selling the car within the motor trade. In April 2019 the V5C form was updated, so forms issued after this date will look slightly different.

Previous ownership records

Due to the introduction of important new legislation on data protection, it is no longer possible to acquire, from the British DVLA, a list of previous owners of a car you own, or are intending to purchase. This scenario will also apply to dealerships and other specialists, from whom you may wish to make contact and acquire information on previous ownership and work carried out.

Roadworthiness certificate

Most country/state administrations require that vehicles are regularly tested to prove that they are safe to use on the public highway and do not produce excessive emissions. In the UK that test (the MOT) is carried out at approved testing stations, for a fee. In the US the requirement varies, but most states insist on an emissions test every two years as a minimum, while the police are charged with pulling over unsafe-looking vehicles.

In the UK, the test is required every year once a vehicle becomes three years old. Of particular relevance for older cars is that the certificate issued includes the mileage reading recorded at the test date and, therefore, becomes an independent record of that car's history. Ask the seller if previous certificates are available. If a valid MOT certificate is not supplied, you should get the vehicle trailered to its new home, unless you insist that a valid MOT is part of the deal. (Not such a bad idea this, as at least you will know the car was roadworthy on the day it was tested and you don't need to wait for the old certificate to expire before having the test done.)

Road licence

The administration of nearly every country/state charges some kind of tax for the use of its road system, the actual form of the 'road licence' and, how it is displayed, varying enormously country to country and state to state.

Whatever the form of the 'road licence,' it must relate to the vehicle carrying it and must be present and valid if the car is to be driven on the public highway legally. The value of the licence will depend on the length of time it will continue to be valid.

Changed legislation in the UK means that the seller of a car must surrender any existing road fund licence, and it is the responsibility of the new owner to re-tax the vehicle at the time of purchase and before the car can be driven on the road. It's therefore vital to see the Vehicle Registration Certificate (V5C) at the time of purchase, and to have access to the New Keeper Supplement (V5C/2), allowing the buyer to obtain road tax immediately.

If the car is untaxed because it has not been used for a period of time, the owner has to inform the licensing authorities, otherwise the vehicle's date-related registration number will be lost and there will be a painful amount of paperwork to get it re-registered.

Valuation certificate

A private vendor may have a recent valuation certificate, or letter signed by a recognised expert stating how much he, or she, believes the particular car to be worth (such documents, together with photos, are usually needed to get 'agreed value' insurance). Generally, such documents should act only as confirmation of your own assessment of the car rather than a guarantee of value. The easiest way to find out how to obtain a formal valuation is to contact the owners' club.

Service history

Try to obtain as much service history and other paperwork pertaining to the car as you can. Naturally, dealer stamps, or specialist garage receipts score most points in the value stakes. However, anything helps in the great authenticity game, items like the original bill of sale, handbook, parts invoices and repair bills adding to the story and the character of the car. Even a brochure correct to the year of the car's manufacture is a useful document and something that you could well have to search hard to locate in future years. If the seller claims that the car has been restored, then expect receipts and other evidence from a specialist restorer.

If the seller claims to have carried out regular servicing, ask what work was completed, when, and seek some evidence of it being carried out. Your assessment of the car's overall condition should tell you whether the seller's claims are genuine.

Restoration photographs

If the seller tells you that the car has undergone significant work, ask to be shown a series of photographs taken while the work was under way. These should help you gauge the thoroughness of the work. If you buy the car, ask if you can have all the photographs, as they form an important part of the vehicle's history. It's surprising how many sellers are happy to part with their car and accept your cash but want to hang on to their photographs! In the latter event, you may be able to persuade the vendor to get a set of copies made.

12 What's it worth?
– let your head rule your heart

Condition

If the car you've been looking at is really bad, then you've probably not bothered to use the marking system in Chapter 9 – the 60-minute evaluation. You may not have even got as far as using that chapter at all!

If you did use the marking system in Chapter 9, you'll know whether the car is in Excellent (maybe concours), Good, Average or Poor condition or, perhaps, somewhere in between these categories. Many car magazines run a regular price guide (not always accurate to current market prices). If you haven't bought the latest editions, do so now and compare their suggested values for the model you are thinking of buying; also look at the auction prices they're reporting. The values published tend to vary from one magazine to another, as do their scales of condition, so read carefully the guidance notes they provide. Bear in mind that a recent show winner could be worth more than the highest scale published. Assuming that the car you have in mind is not in show/concours condition, then relate the level of condition that you judge the car to be in with the appropriate guide price. How does the figure compare with the asking price? Before you start haggling with the seller, consider what effect any variation from standard specification might have on the car's value. If you are buying from a dealer, remember there will be a dealer's premium on the price. Finally, values of integrale are climbing strongly, so don't wait too long!

The Dealers Collection version had many desirable features: leather interior, push button ignition switch, white dial surround and passenger rally foot rest.
(Courtesy Justin Narillo)

Desirable options/extras

For 16v integrale to Evo I, leather and air-conditioning were offered as an optional package. In some markets, for example Italy, you could also have a sunroof as part of this option. This was not permitted in the UK, you had to choose either the sunroof or the leather and air con option. German spec cars had manual sunroofs and check panel as standard. There were not many optional extras available as the cars were already well equipped, and some of the last Evo II models which were limited editions had leather interior fitted as standard.

The hi-fi club edition had tailored and colour coded luggage supplied with the car.

Undesirable features

Some aftermarket steering wheels, gearlever tops, instrument surrounds or pedals may have been added – these do not add to the value or desirability of the car, and may even lessen the value. Also, you might find a later Evo model rear spoiler fitted to an earlier version of the car. Original features are generally more desirable.

13 Do you really want to restore?
– it'll take longer and cost more than you think

It is most likely that a car needing restoration will either be a badly treated example, a rally car or one used for club competition. You may be tempted to restore a car from scratch, or buy one that was first restored, perhaps to lower standards a few years ago. If you do decide to take on a restoration project, check carefully when viewing a car to see which parts come with it: the more complete it is, the better! Apart from the cost of some items, bear in mind the time you may need to track down hard-to-find parts. If you go ahead, be sure to take plenty of photographs documenting the work you have done.

In nearly every case, however, buying a car to restore will be a decision made with the heart rather than the head: integrale prices haven't climbed to the point where a 'cost no object' restoration can be done and a profit added (except certain Evo limited editions). If you are not doing it all yourself, specialists' labour costs will soon add up. There are certain qualified restoration businesses operating in Italy which can cost less, and where parts are more readily available.

The Martini 6 limited edition: the closest look to the factory rally cars on a road version.

Integrales are mainly painted in base colours. Reds from any manufacturer are known to fade. Do not be surprised to find glass fibre or plastic panels to be a slightly different colour and finish to steel or aluminium. Paint faults generally occur due to lack of protection/maintenance, or to poor preparation prior to a respray or touch-up. Measuring the paint depth on each panel will help confirm if all the paint is original. Some of the following conditions may be present in the car you're looking at.

Orange peel
This appears as an uneven paint surface, similar to the skin of an orange. This fault is caused by the failure of atomised paint droplets to flow into each other when they hit the surface. It's sometimes possible to rub out the effect with proprietary paint cutting/ rubbing compound, or very fine grades of abrasive paper. A respray may be necessary in severe cases. Consult a bodywork repairer/paint shop for advice on the particular car.

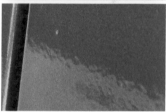

Orange peel.

Cracking
Severe cases are likely to have been caused by too heavy an application of paint (or filler beneath the paint). Also, insufficient stirring of the paint before application can lead to the components being improperly mixed, and cracking can result. Incompatibility with the paint already on the panel can have a similar effect. To rectify the problem, it is necessary to rub down to a smooth, sound finish before respraying the problem area.

Crazing
Sometimes the paint takes on a crazed rather than a cracked appearance when the problems mentioned under 'Cracking' are

Cracking and crazing.

present. This problem can also be caused by a reaction between the underlying surface and the paint. Paint removal and respraying the problem area is usually the only solution.

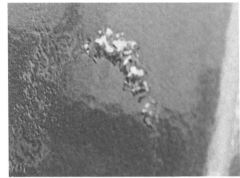

Paint reaction.

Blistering
Almost always caused by corrosion of the metal beneath the paint. Usually perforation will be found in the metal and the damage will usually be worse than that suggested by the area of blistering. The metal will have to be repaired before repainting.

Fading
Some colours, especially reds, are prone to fading if subjected to strong sunlight for long periods without the benefit of polish protection. Sometimes proprietary paint restorers and/or paint cutting/rubbing compounds will retrieve the situation. Often a respray is the only real solution.

Micro blistering
Usually the result of an economy respray where inadequate heating has allowed moisture to settle on the car before spraying. Consult a paint specialist, but usually damaged paint will have to be removed before partial or full respraying. Can also be caused by car covers that don't 'breathe.'

Micro blistering.

Peeling
Often a problem with metallic paintwork when the sealing lacquer becomes damaged and begins to peel off. Poorly applied paint may also peel. The remedy is to strip and start again!

Dimples
Dimples in the paintwork are caused by the residue of polish (particularly silicone types) not being removed properly before respraying. Paint removal and repainting is the only solution.

Dents
Small dents are usually easily cured by the 'Dentmaster' or equivalent process, that sucks or pushes out the dent (as long as the paint surface is still intact). Companies offering dent removal services usually come to your home: consult your telephone directory or search online.

15 Problems due to lack of use

– just like their owners, HF 4WDs and integrales need exercise!

Cars, like humans, are at their most efficient if they exercise regularly. A run of at least ten miles, once a week, is recommended for all older cars.

Seized components
Pistons in callipers, slave and master cylinders can seize. The clutch may seize if the plate becomes stuck to the flywheel because of corrosion. Handbrakes (parking brakes) can seize if the cables and linkages rust. Pistons can seize in the bores due to corrosion.

Fluids
Old, acidic oil can corrode bearings. Uninhibited coolant can corrode internal waterways. Lack of antifreeze can cause core plugs to be pushed out, even cracks in the block or head. Silt settling and solidifying can cause overheating. Brake fluid absorbs water from the atmosphere and should be renewed every two years. Old fluid with a high water content can cause corrosion and pistons/calipers to seize (freeze) and can cause brake failure when the water turns to vapour near hot braking components,

Tyre problems
Tyres that have had the weight of the car on them in a single position for some time will develop flat spots, resulting in some (usually temporary) vibration. The tyre walls may have cracks or (blister-type) bulges, meaning new tyres are needed.

Shock absorbers (dampers)
With lack of use, the dampers will lose their elasticity or even seize. Creaking, groaning and stiff suspension are signs of this problem. Ride height can also drop.

Rubber and plastic
Radiator hoses may have perished and split, possibly resulting in the loss of all coolant. Window and door seals can harden and leak. Gaitors/boots can crack. Wiper blades will harden.

Electrics
The battery will be of little use if it has not been charged for many months. Earthing/grounding problems are common when the connections have corroded. Old bullet and spade type electrical connectors commonly rust/corrode and will need disconnecting, cleaning and protection (eg: Vaseline). Sparkplug electrodes will often have corroded in an unused engine. Wiring insulation can harden and fail. Dashboard lights can also dim over age and time, and the rheostat even when up to max does not always add enough brightness.

Rotting exhaust system
Exhaust gas contains a high water content, so exhaust systems corrode very quickly from the inside when the car is not used.

16 The Community
– key people, organisations and companies in the Lancia world

It is a good idea to join a club where there are other people with experience and a shared love of this car. There are numerous clubs worldwide, as well as internet forums and Facebook groups, which can help with advice and parts availability etc.

The oldest Lancia club in the world is in the UK; it caters for all Lancia cars, and can be found online at Lanciamotorclub.co.uk. As a vice president of this club with a 30-year history of ownership, I am available to help owners and prospective owners.

Parts availability

Many parts have been sold out for some years, and are almost impossible to get, unless you find someone who has stockpiled.

Things like rear quarter panels, bonnets, front wings (Evo wings are one piece items where as the 8 & 16v versions had add on extensions), headlamps, probably too many to list here, but suppliers usually have stock of most service items.

At time of writing, FCA and MOPAR have announced that they are remaking integrale bumpers at a cost of approximately £2300 for a pair, which is great news, and hopefully this is the start of many parts being remanufactured.

List of recommended parts suppliers

Tanc Barrett UK   www.projoe.nl
www.DeltaParts.de   www.Billstein.de

Servicing

Neil Boggas: Project Lancia, Sawbridgeworth Herts: 07949 968587
Neil is ex-John Whalley, and is fully experienced on Deltas for over 30 years, as well as being Alfa Romeo trained.

Keith Turner: Auto integral, Reading, Berks, 0118 9710186
Keith has been working on these cars for over 30 years, and has a vast knowledge and experience.

AutoCasa Coventry: 0247 767 8535
Business run by owners and enthusiasts of the Delta HF. Enzo Licata is very knowledgeable, with attention to detail being paramount in the company's ethos.

Adam Atfield: 07771 560741
Ex-Jack Rose Lancia main dealer mechanic, experienced on Deltas. Sourcing Recommissioning and Restoration.

Omologato Consultancy: www.omologatoconsultancy.com
This company has excellent links to specialists in Italy, who built the cars originally, and can project manage restoration or recommissioning work carried out by ex-Abarth mechanics and engineers. It can also provide history checks on Group A and Group B rally cars, and inspections can be carried out. If you are seeking to find a particular car, they can assist you and offer advice.

17 Vital statistics
– essential data at your fingertips

Editions and variants

Model	Code	Engine code	Number produced
HF 4WD (86-87)	831ABO19	B5.000	5298
8v integrale (87-89)	831ABO24	C5.000	9841
8v KAT (Swiss) (89-91)	831ABO024S	C5.046	2700
16v integrale (89-91)	831ABO026	D5.000	12,860
Evo I (91-92)	831ABO027	E5.000	4841
Evo I KAT (Swiss) (91-92)	831ABO028	E5.046	4650
Evo II (93-95)	831ABO029	E5.046	1224

Cutaway drawing of the
Lancia Delta HF integrale.

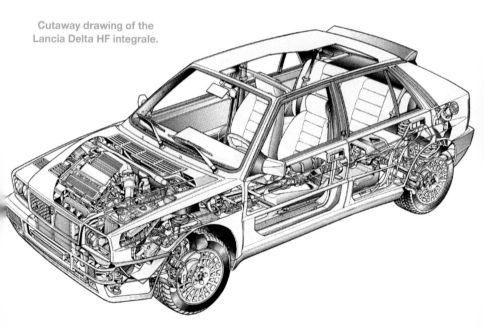

Lancia Delta HF integrale 8v specifications (pages 66-71)

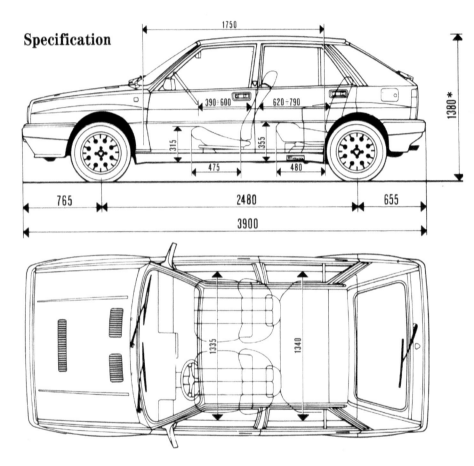

Luggage compartment capacity: 200 dm³, with the rear seat folded over: 940 dm³.

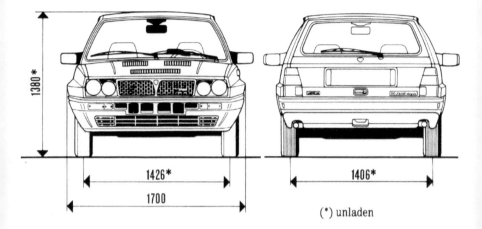

(*) unladen

ENGINE

Main features

No. of cylinders	4 in line
Cycle-stroke	Otto-4
Bore x stroke	87 × 90 mm
Cylinder capacity	1,995 cc.
Compression ratio	8 to 1
Max power output	185 bhp-DIN
	5,300 rpm
Max torque (EEC)	31 mkg-DIN
at	2500 rpm - 2750 rpm
Fuel required	Premium, 4-Star

Structural layout

Arrangement	transversely-mounted at front
Cylinder spacings	91 mm
Main bearings	5
Cylinder head	light alloy
Cylinder block	cast iron with counter-rotating balancer shafts

Timing gear

Valve arrangement	at V(65°)
Camshafts	2 overhead

Timing control	by toothed belt
Phasing	phasing control play = 0.8 mm

Intake	\ beginning	8° before TDC
	/ end	42° after BDC
Exhaust	\ beginning	42° before BDC
	/ end	1° after TDC
Counter-rotating balancer shafts		2 in the cylinder block
Control		by toothed belt

Ignition

Type	electronic with mapped advance control and knock sensor, combined with the injection
Firing order	1-3-4-2
Spark plugs	Marelli F8LCR - Fiat/Lancia V45LSR Champion RN7YC - Bosch WR6DC

Fuel feed

Type	supercharging by turbocharger and air/air heat exchanger off the ignition and overboost automatically engaged at full revs
Fuel pump	electric
Injection	electronic IAW Weber combined with the ignition
Air cleaner	dry-type, with paper cardridge
Turboblower type	water-cooled Garrett T3
Max supercharging pressure	1.0 bar

Lubrication

Type	forced feed with gear pump and oil radiator
Oil filter	gear-type

Engine cooling

Type	water-forced by pump with radiator and additional expansion tank
Control	thermostat
Fan	electric, controlled from a thermostatic switch on the radiator

TRANSMISSION

Type	permanent 4 wheel drive with centrally-mounted epicyclic torque converter and Ferguson viscous joint; Torsen-type rear differential with 5 to 1 wheel torque ratio
Clutch	dry, single plate
Friction ring diameter $(Ø_e × Ø_i)$	230 × 155 mm

Transmission ratios:

1st	3.500 : 1
2nd	2.235 : 1
3rd	1.518 : 1
4th	1.132 : 1
5th	0.928 : 1
Reverse	3.583 : 1
Final drive ratio	3.111 : 1 (55/18)

Bevel gear front/rear	2.263 : 1 (19/43)
Torque converter { front / rear	56% / 44%

Body   self-bearing structure

Braking system   front and rear discs with floating
                                  calipers, diagonal-split type hydraulic
                                  brake circuit with vacuum servo and
                                  brake effort proportioning valve acting
                                  on the rear wheels

CHASSIS

Front discs	
- diameter	284 mm (self-ventilating)
- total front brake linings	50 × 4 = 200 cm²
Rear discs	
- diameter	227 mm
- total rear brake linings	35 × 4 = 140 cm²
Parking brake	acting on the shoes of the rear discs

Front suspension   independent MacPherson-type struts,
                                 lower wishbones, anti-roll bar, and
                                 double-acting hydraulic telescopic
                                 dampers

Flexibility at the wheel	0.55 mm/kg
Wheel wobble { upper / lower	78 mm / 85 mm
Wheel position (unladen)	
- camber	– 40' ± 30'
- caster	2°50' ± 30'
- toe-in	– 2 ÷ 1.5

Rear suspension   independent MacPherson-type struts,
                                 transverse links, longitudinal reaction
                                 rods and anti-roll bar

Flexibility at the wheel	0.55 mm/kg
Wheel wobble { upper / lower	75 mm / 125 mm
Wheel position (unladen)	
- camber	– 55' ± 30'
- caster	2°25' ± 30'
- toe-in	32 to 5 mm

Steering   servo-assisted rack and pinion
Turning circle   10.4 m
Steering wheel turns lock to lock 2.8

Road wheels
Rims   light alloy 6 × 15"
Tyres   195/55 VR 15
Inflating pressure
- front   2.0 bar - 2.2 bar (**)
- rear   2.0 bar - 2.2 bar (**)

Spare wheel

Rim	light alloy 4J × 15" AH2-40
Tyre	115 × 70 R15
Inflating pressure front/rear	4.2 bar

(**) at high constant speed, fully laden

Electrical equipment

Voltage	12 V
Alternator with built-in electronic voltage regulator	65 A
Starter motor	1.1 kW
Battery	45 Ah (service free)

WEIGHTS

Kerb weight (DIN)*	1,200 kg (2,645 lbs)
Distribution \ front	63%
/ rear	37%
Laden weight	1,665 kg
Distribution \ front	54.7%
/ rear	45.3%
Maximum payload	450 kg
Max towing weight	1,200 kg
No. of seats	5

(*) Inclusive of fuel, water, spare wheel, and accessories.

PERFORMANCE

Top speed (in 5th)	215 km/h (133 mph)
Max gradient climbable (laden)	58%
Speed at 1,000 rpm \ in 4th	30.9 km/h
/ in 5th	37.7 km/h
Power/weight ratio kg/bhp	6.57

Acceleration

(2 adults + 20 kg)	(secs)
0 ÷ 100 km/h (0-62 mph)	6.6 s
0 ÷ 400 m	14.7 s
0 ÷ 1,000 m	27.1 s

Pickup from 40 km/h (in 5th)

(2 adults + 20 kg)	(secs)
over 1,000 m	36 s
over 400 m	20.2 s
40 ÷ 100 km/h	20.0 s

Conventional fuel consumption

	(l/100 km)	(mpg)
at 90 km/h	7.7	36.7
at 120 km/h	10.2	27.7
urban cycle	10.8	26.2
ECE average	9.6	29.4

SUPPLIES

	dm³	kg
Fuel tank capacity	57 (12.5 gals)	–
including a reserve of:	6 to 9 (1.3-2 gals)	–
Engine radiator, expansion tank, and heating system liquid	6.20	–
Oil pan	4.9	4.4
Total capacity of pan filter, radiator and ducting oil	5.9	5.2
Gearbox and differential oil	3.8	3.4
Rear differential	1.1	1
Power-steering box grease	0.68	0.61
Hydraulic brake circuits liquid	0.30	0.29
Wind-screen and rear screen washer bottle	2.0	–

Lancia Delta HF integrale 16v specifications (pages 71-77)

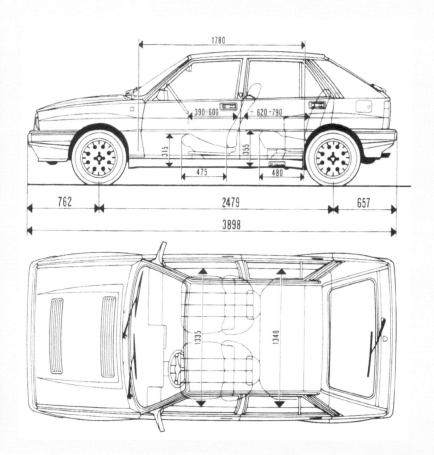

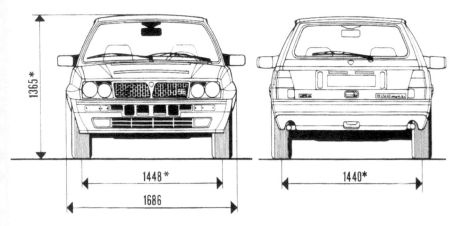

Luggage compartment capacity: 200 dm³; with the rear seat folded over: 940 dm³.

ENGINE

Main features

No. of cylinders	4 flat
Cycle-stroke	petrol-fed
Bore x stroke	84 × 90 mm
Cylinder capacity	1995 cc
Compression ratio	8 to 1
Max power output DIN	200 bhp (144 kW-EEC)
	5500 rpm
Peak at torque DIN	31 mkg (298 Nm-EEC)
at	3000 rpm
Octane	leaded or unleaded petrol; lowest octane rating 95 (RON)

Structural layout

Arrangement	transversely-mounted at front
Cylinder block	cast iron with counter-rotating balancer shafts
Cylinder spacings	91 mm
Main bearings	5
Cylinder head	light alloy

Timing gear

Valve arrangement	at V(65°)
Camshafts	2 overhead
Timing control	by toothed belt
Phasing	phasing control play = 0.8 mm
Intake { beginning	8° before TDC
end	35° after BDC
Exhaust { beginning	30° before BDC
end	0° after TDC
Counter-rotating balancer shafts	2 in the cylinder block
Control	by toothed belt

Ignition

Type	electronic with mapped advance control and knock sensor, combined with the injection
Firing order	1-3-4-2
Spark plugs	Champion RN7YC - Bosch WR6DC - Marelli F8LCR - FIAT-LANCIA V45LSR

Fuel feed

Type	turbocharging and air/air heat exchanger (off the intake) and overboost automatically engaging at full engine revs
Fuel pump	electric
Injection	electronic IAW Weber combined with the ignition
Air cleaner	dry-type, with paper cartridge
Turboblower type	water-cooled Garrett T3
Max turbocharging pressure	1 bar

Lubrication

Type	forced feed with gear pump and oil radiator
Filter	cartridge-type

Engine cooling

Type	water-forced with radiator pump and extra expansion tank
Control	by thermostat
Fan	electric, controlled from a thermostatic switch on the radiator

TRANSMISSION

Type	permanent 4-wheel drive with centrally-mounted epicyclic torque converter and Ferguson viscous coupling; Torsen-type rear differential with 5 to 1 wheel torque ratio

Clutch	dry, single plate, hydraulically controlled
Friction ring diameter ($\varnothing_e \times \varnothing_i$)	230 × 155 mm

Transmission ratios:

Gearbox	
1st	3.500 : 1
2nd	2.176 : 1
3rd	1.519 : 1
4th	1.132 : 1
5th	0.929 : 1
Reverse	3.545 : 1
Final drive ratio	3.111 : 1 (56/18)
Bevel gear front/rear	2.263 : 1 (19/43)
Torque splitter { front	47%
{ rear	53%

CHASSIS

Body — self-bearing structure

Braking system — front and rear discs with floating calipers. Diagonal-split type hydraulic brake circuit with vacuum servo and brake-effort proportioning valve acting on the rear wheels. Antilock Braking System (ABS) optionally available.

Front discs	
– diameter	284 mm (ventilated)
– total front pad area	50 × 4 = 200 cm²
Rear discs	
– diameter	227 mm
– total rear pad area	35 × 4 = 140 cm²
Parking brake	acting on the discs of the rear brakes

Front suspension — independent wheel struts with lower wishbones, anti-roll bar and double-acting hydraulic telescopic gas-operated dampers

Flexibility at the wheel	0.50 mm/kg
Wheel wobble { upper	60 mm
{ lower	103 mm
Wheel position (unladen)	
– camber	– 1° ± 30'

- caster	3°10' ± 30'
- toe-in	- 2 to +1 mm

Rear suspension

independent wheel struts with transverse links, longitudinal reaction arms, anti-roll bar and hydraulic, telescopic double-acting gas-operated dampers

Flexibility at the wheel	0.51 mm/kg
Wheel wobble { upper	60 mm
{ lower	125 mm
Wheel position (unladen)	
- camber	- 1°30' ± 30'
- caster	2°30' ± 30'
- toe-in	3 to 5 mm

Steering

servo-assisted rack-and-pinion power steering

Turning circle	10.4 m
Steering wheel turns lock to lock	2.8

Road wheels

Rims	light alloy 7 J × 15"
Tyres	205/50 R 15 V
Inflating pressure	
- front	2.0 bar - (2.2 bar**)
- rear	2.0 bar - (2.2 bar**)

Spare wheel

Rim	light alloy 4J × 15" AH2-40
Tyre	115 × 70 R15
Inflating pressure	4.2 bar

(**) at high constant speed, fully laden

Electrical equipment

Voltage	12 V
Alternator with built-in voltage regulator	65 A
Starter motor	1.1 kW
Battery	45 Ah (service free)

WEIGHTS

Kerb weight (DIN)*	1250 kg
Distribution { front	62.4%
{ rear	37.6%
Laden weight	1700 kg
Distribution { front	53.5%
{ rear	46.5%

Maximum payload	450 kg
Max towing weight	1300 kg
No. of seats	5

(*) Inclusive of fuel, water, spare wheel and accessories.

PERFORMANCE

Top speed in 5th	220 km/h (80 km/h) (*)
Max gradient climbable (laden)	58%
Speed at 1000 rpm ⎰ in 4th	30.6 km/h
⎱ in 5th	37.3 km/h
Power-to-weight ratio ⎰ kg/bhp-DIN	6.25
⎱ kg/kW-EEC	8.7

(*) Max permissible speed when mounting the low-section spare wheel

Acceleration
(2 adults + 20 kg) (secs)

0 to 100 km/h	5.7 s
0 to 1000 m	26.1 s

Pic-kup from 40 km/h in 5th
(2 adults + 20 kg) (secs)

over 1000 m	30.5 s

**Conventional fuel consumption
(l/100 km):**

at 90 km/h	7.9
at 120 km/h	10.5
urban cycle	11.2
ECE mean	9

SUPPLIES

	dm³	kg
Fuel tank capacity	57	–
including a reserve of:	6 to 9	–
Engine radiator, expansion tank and heating system liquid	6.2	–
Oil pan	4.9	4.4
Total capacity of pan, filter, radiator and ducting oil	5.8	5.2
Gearbox and differential oil	3.8	3.4
Rear differential	1.1	1
Servo-assisted power-steering	0.75	–
Hydraulic brake circuits liquid	0.40	–
Wind- and rear-screen washer bottle	2	–

CHARACTERISTIC ENGINE CURVES (EEC)

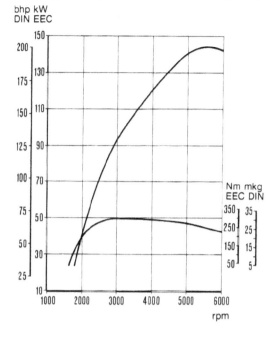

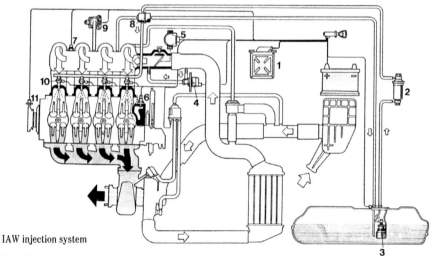

IAW injection system

1) injection/ignition central control unit;
2) fuel filtre;
3) electric fuel filtre;
4) air valve;
5) potentiometer sensor of throttle-valve position;
6) engine coolant temperature sensor;
6) engine coolant temperature sensor;
7) inlet air temperature sensor;
8) boost control;
9) absolute atmospheric pressure sensor;
10) electro-injectors;
11) crankshaft location and rotation-speed sensor.

Specification

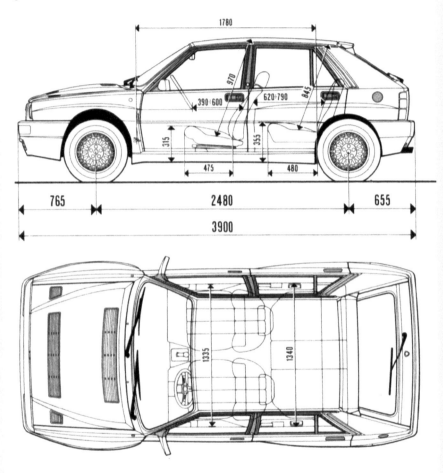

Luggage compartment capacity: 200 dm^3; with back seat folded down: 940 dm^3

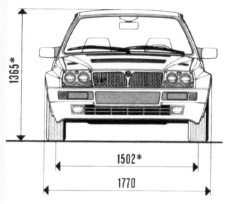

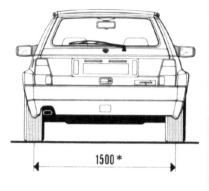

* unladen

ENGINE

Main features

No. cylinders	4, in line
Cycle-stroke	Otto-4
Bore × stroke	84 × 90 mm
Displacement	1995 cc
Compression ratio	8 : 1
Max. power output DIN	210 bhp (151 kW - EEC)
at	5750 rpm
Peak torque DIN	31 mkg (298 Nm - EEC)
at	3500 rpm
Fuel	leaded or unleaded petrol (RON 95)

Construction

Layout	front transverse
Cylinder block	cast iron with counter-rotating balancer shafts
Cylinder spacings	91 mm
No. of main bearings	5
Cylinder head	light alloy

Timing

Valve arrangement	at V (65°)
Timing	DOHC

Timing control	toothed belt
Timing	0.8 mm timing control tolerance
Inlet { Opens	8° BTDC
Closes	35° ABDC
Exhaust { Opens	30° BBDC
Closes	0° ATDC
Counter-rotating balancer shafts	2 in the cylinder block
Control	by toothed belt

Ignition

Type	electronic with mapped advance and knock sensor, combined with the injection
Firing order	1-3-4-2
Spark plugs	Bosch WR6DTC

Fuel feed

Type	supercharging by turbocharger and air/air heat exchanger on intake and overboost (automatically engaged at full revs)
Fuel pump	electric
Injection	electronic IAW Weber combined with the ignition
Air cleaner	dry-type, with paper cartridge
Turboblower: type	water-cooled Garrett T3
Max supercharging pressure	1 bar

Lubrication

Type	forced feed with gear pump and oil radiator
Oil filter	cartridge

Engine cooling

Type	water-forced by pump with radiator and additional expansion tank
Control	thermostat
Fan	electric, controlled from a thermostatic switch on the radiator

TRANSMISSION

Power drive: type	permanent 4 wheel drive with centre differential, epicyclic torque converter and Ferguson viscous joint; Torsen-type rear differential with 5 to 1 wheel torque ratio
Clutch	dry, single plate, hydraulically controlled
Friction ring diameter (o.d. × i.d.)	230 × 155 mm

Transmission ratios

Gearbox

1st	3.500:1
2nd	2.176:1
3rd	1.523:1
4th	1.156:1
5th	0.916:1
Reverse	3.545:1
Final drive ratio	3.111:1 (18/56)
Bevel gear front/rear	2.263:1 (19/43)
Torque splitter	$\begin{cases} \text{front: 47\%} \\ \text{rear: 53\%} \end{cases}$

CHASSIS

Body — self-bearing structure

Braking system — front and rear discs with double cylinder front and rear floating calipers, diagonal-split type hydraulic brake circuit with vacuum servo and brake effort proportioning valve acting on the rear wheels. Optionally available: ABS

Front discs
— diameter — 281 mm (self-ventilating)
— total front brake linings — $54 \times 4 = 216 \text{ cm}^2$

Rear discs
— diameter — 251 mm
— total rear brake linings — $35 \times 4 = 140 \text{ cm}^2$
Parking brake — acting on the rear brake discs

Front suspension — independent MacPherson-type struts, lower wishbones, anti-roll bar, and double-acting gas-type hydraulic telescopic dampers

Flexibility at the wheel — 0.50 mm/kg

Wheel wobble $\begin{cases} \text{upper} \\ \text{lower} \end{cases}$ — 60 mm / 103 mm

Wheel position
(unladen)
— camber — $-1° \pm 30'$
— caster — $3°10' \pm 30'$
— toe-in — $-2 - +1$ mm

Rear suspension — independent MacPherson-type struts, transverse links, longitudinal reaction rods, anti-roll bar and double-acting gas-type hydraulic telescopic dampers

Flexibility at the wheel — 0.51 mm/kg

Wheel wobble $\begin{cases} \text{upper} \\ \text{lower} \end{cases}$ — 60 mm / 125 mm

Wheel position
(unladen)
— camber $-1°30' \pm 30'$
— caster $2°30' \pm 30'$
— toe-in   3 - 5 mm

Steering   rack and pinion power steering
Turning circle   10.4 m
Steering wheel turns lock to lock   2.8

Road wheels
Rims   light alloy: $7\frac{1}{2} J \times 15''$
Tyres   205/50 ZR 15
Inflation pressure
— front   2.2 bar (2.5 bar**)
— rear   2.2 bar (2.5 bar**)

Spare wheel
Rim   light alloy: $3\frac{1}{2} B \times 16''$ H2-37
Tyre   T115/70 R 16
Inflation pressure   4.2 bar (front and rear)
Top speed permitted   80 km/h
(**) at high constant speed, fully laden

Electrical equipment
Voltage   12 V
Alternator with built-in electronic
voltage regulator   65 A
Starter motor   1.1 kW
Battery capacity   45 Ah (service free)

WEIGHTS

Kerb weight (DIN)*   1300 kg
Distribution $\begin{cases} \text{front} \\ \text{rear} \end{cases}$ 62.4%
          37.6%
Laden weight   1750 kg
Max. weight permitted $\begin{cases} \text{front} \\ \text{rear} \end{cases}$ 1030 kg
          1030 kg
Maximum payload   450 kg
Max towing weight   1300 kg
No. of seats   5
(*) Inclusive of fuel, water, spare wheel, and accessories.

PERFORMANCE

Top speed (in 5th)   220 km/h
Max gradient climbable
(laden)   58%
Speed $\begin{cases} \text{in 4th} \\ \text{in 5th} \end{cases}$ 30.3
at 1,000 rpm   38.2
Power/weight ratio $\begin{cases} \text{kg/bhp-DIN} \\ \text{kg/kW-EEC} \end{cases}$ 6.19
          8.6

Acceleration (2 adults + 20 kg) (secs)
0-100 km/h	5.7
0-1000 m	26.1

Pickup from 40 km/h (in 4th)
(2 adults + 20 kg) (secs)
over 1000 m	30.5

Conventional fuel consumption (l/100 km)
at 90 km/h	7.9
at 120 km/h	10.5
urban cycle	11.2
ECE average	9

SUPPLIES

	dm³ (l)	kg
Fuel tank capacity	57	—
including a reserve of:	6 to 9	—
Engine radiator, expansion tank, and heating system liquid	6.2	—
Oil Sump	4.9	4.4
Total capacity of Sump filter, radiator and ducting oil	5.8	5.2
Gearbox and differential, oil	3.8	3.4
Rear differential	1.1	1
Power-steering box	0.75	—
Hydraulic brake circuits liquid	0.40	—
Wind-screen and rear screen washer bottle	2	—

CHARACTERISTIC ENGINE CURVES (EEC)

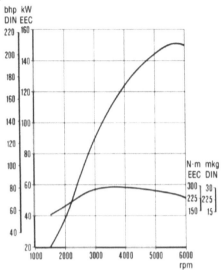

Cutaway drawing showing the HF integrale 4x4 transmission.

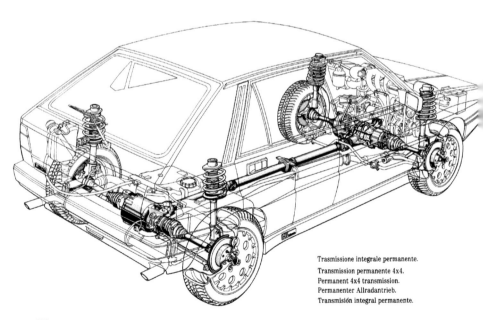

Trasmissione integrale permanente.
Transmission permanente 4x4.
Permanent 4x4 transmission.
Permanenter Allradantrieb.
Transmisión integral permanente.

* unladen

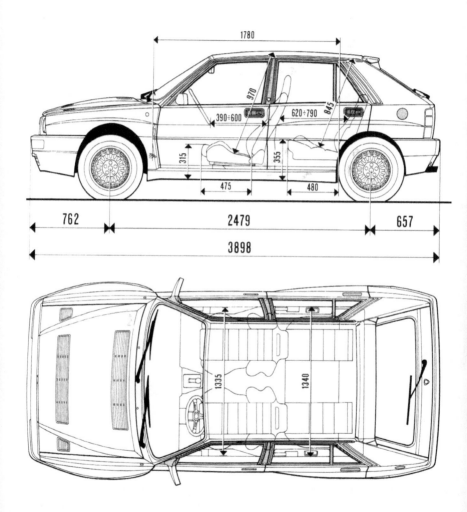

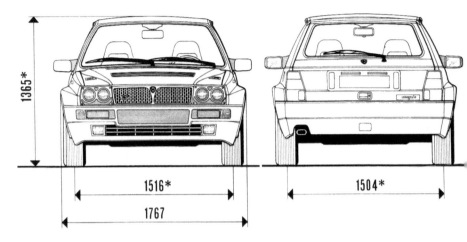

Boot capacity: 200 dm³; with rear seat folded: 940 dm³

ENGINE

Main features
No. of cylinders	4, in line
Cycle-stroke	Otto-4
Bore x stroke	84 × 90 mm
Displacement	1995 cc
Compression ratio	8:1
Max power output DIN	215 bhp (155 kW-EEC)
at	5750 rpm
Peak torque DIN	32 mkg (308 Nm-EEC)
at	2500 rpm
Fuel required	unleaded petrol (95 RON)

Structure
Position	front transverse
Cylinder block	cast iron, with counter-rotating shafts
Cylinder spacing	91 mm
Main bearings	5
Cylinder head	light alloy

Timing gear

Position/No. of valves	V (65°)/4 per cylinder
Timing	DOHC
Timing control	toothed belt
Valve gear timing	with tappet play of 0.8 mm
Intake opens	8° BTDC
closes	35° ABDC
Exhaust opens	30° BBDC
closes	0° ATDC
No. of counter-rotating shafts	2 in cylinder block

Ignition

Type	electronic mapped advance, knock sensor, integrated with injection
Fire order	1-3-4-2
Spark plugs	Bosch WR6DTC

Fuel feed

	turbocharged with turbocompressor and air/air heat exchanger on intake + overboost (and automatic cut-in with engine at full revs)
Petrol pump	electric
Injection: type	IAW electronic MPI combined with ignition
Air filter	dry-type with paper cartridge
Turbocharger: type	Garrett T3, water cooled
Max. boost pressure	1 bar

Lubrication

Type	forced-feed, geared pump, with oil radiator
Filter	cartridge

Cooling

Type	liquid, with pressurised circuit, radiator pump and supplementary expansion tank
Control	by thermostat
Fan	electric, controlled by a thermostatic switch on the radiator

Emission control

three-way catalytic converter, lambda sensor

TRANSMISSION

Drive: type   permanent four-wheel with central differential, epicyclic torque splitter and Ferguson viscous joint;

	Torsen rear differential with 5:1 torque ratio between wheels
Clutch	dry, single plate, with hydraulic control
Friction lining dimensions (OD x ID)	230 × 155 mm

Gear ratios

1st	3.500:1
2nd	2.176:1
3rd	1.523:1
4th	1.156:1
5th	0.916:1
Reverse	3.545:1
Final ratio (spur gear pair)	3.111:1 (18/56)
Front and rear bevel gear pair	2.263:1 (19/43)
Torque split	front: 47% rear: 53%

CHASSIS

Body	stress-bearing
Braking system	discs front and rear with double cylinder front calipers and floating calipers at rear. Pedal control, with vacuum servo, two independent diagonally split hydraulic circuits, and load proportioning valve on rear wheels. Standard ABS.
Front discs	self-ventilating
- diameter	281 mm
- total lining area	54 × 4 = 216 sq. cm.
Rear discs	
- diameter	251 mm
- total lining area	35 × 4 = 140 sq. cm.
Parking brake	acting on rear brake discs
Front suspension	independent MacPherson struts with transverse lower wishbones and anti-roll bar
Dampers	dual action hydraulic, gas telescopic
Flexibility at the wheel	0.50 mm/kg
Wheel wobble upper	60 mm
lower	103 mm
Front wheel geometry unladen	
– camber	– 1° ± 30'
– caster	4°10' ± 30'
– toe-in	– 1 ± 1 mm
Rear suspension	MacPherson independent type with trailing arms, longitudinal reaction bars and anti-roll bar

Dampers	dual action hydraulic, gas telescopic
Flexibility at the wheel	0.51 mm/kg

Wheel wobble	upper	60 mm
	lower	125 mm

Rear wheel geometry
unladen
– camber	– 1°30' ± 30'
– caster	2°30' ± 30'
– toe-in	3 – 5 mm

Steering
Turning circle	rack and pinion, with power steering
Turning circle	10.4 m
Steering wheel turns lock to lock	2.8

Wheels
Rims	7 ¹/₂ J × 16", light alloy
Tyres	205/45 ZR 16

Inflation pressure
– front	2.2 bar (2.5 bar*)
– rear	2.2 bar (2.5 bar*)

(*) continuous high speed, fully laden

Spare wheel
Rim	3 ¹/₂ B × 16" H2-37, light alloy
Tyre	T115/70 R 16
Inflation pressure	4.2 bar (front and rear)
Max. speed permitted	80 km/h

Electrical equipment
Voltage	12 V
Alternator (with incorporated electronic voltage regulator)	65 A
Starter motor	1.1 kW
Battery: capacity	110Ah

WEIGHTS
Kerb weight (DIN) (*)
		1340 kg

Distribution	front	63.3%
	rear	36.7%

Max. permitted weight	front	1020 kg
	rear	1020 kg
	total	1790 kg

Max. payload	450 kg
Max. towing weight	1200 kg
No. of seats	5

(*) Kerb weight (inclusive of fuel, water, spare wheel and accessories)

PERFORMANCE
Max. speed in 5th
		220 km/h

Max. gradient (negotiable
fully laden) | 58%

Speed with engine at 1000 rpm	in 4th	30 km/h
	in 5th	37.9 km/h

| Power to weight ratio | kg/bhp-DIN | 6.2 |
| | kg/kW-EEC | 8.6 |

Accelerations (2 adults + 20 kg) (secs)
| 0 to 100 km/h | 5.7 |
| 0 to 1000 m | 26.1 |

Pick-up from 40 km/h in 4th
(2 adults + 20 kg) (secs)
| 1000 m | 30.5 |

Conventional fuel consumption
(l/100 km)
at 90 km/h	8.2
at 120 km/h	10.6
urban cycle	13
ECE average	10.6

SUPPLIES

	dm³ (l)	kg
Fuel tank	57	–
including a reserve of:	6 – 9	–
Radiator, expansion tank and heating system, fluid	6.2	–
Engine sump and filter, oil	4.9	4.4
Total engine sump, filter and circuit, oil	5.8	5.2
Gearbox and differential oil	3.8	3.4
Rear differential	1.1	1
Power steering	0.75	–
Hydraulic brake tank, liquid	0.52	–
Screenwasher and rear window washer bottle	2	–

CHARACTERISTIC
ENGINE CURVES (EEC)

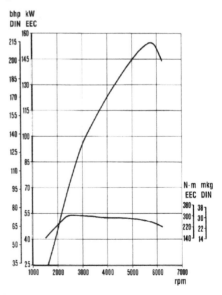

Also available from Veloce

The story of Lancia's mid-engined and supercharged rally car, from its conception, through development, to its full rallying career. Featuring many of Sergio Limone's own comments & photographs, plus interviews with team members. Illustrated with 250 stunning and rare rally action photos.

ISBN: 978-1-787111-28-8
Hardback • 24.6x24.6cm
• 224 pages • 343 colour and b&w pictures

Also available as an ebook.

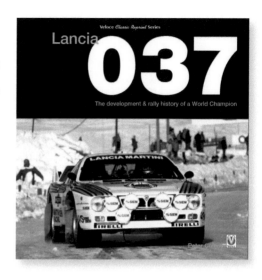

The HF 4WD – a compact, five-door Lancia – dominated world-class rallying for six years, winning innumerable events, World Championships for Drivers, and World Championships for Manufacturers. The Integrale was both the most successful rally car ever produced by Lancia, and the last, for when the car came to the end of its career in 1993, the company finally and irrevocably withdrew from the sport.

ISBN: 978-1-845842-58-1 Paperback • 19.5x21cm
• 128 pages • 108 colour and b&w pictures
Also available as an ebook

For more information and price details, visit our website at www.veloce.co.uk
• email: info@veloce.co.uk • Tel: +44(0)1305 260068

The Essential Buyer's Guide™ series ...

For more details visit:
www.veloce.co.uk
email: info@veloce.co.uk
tel: 01305 260068

Also available from Veloce

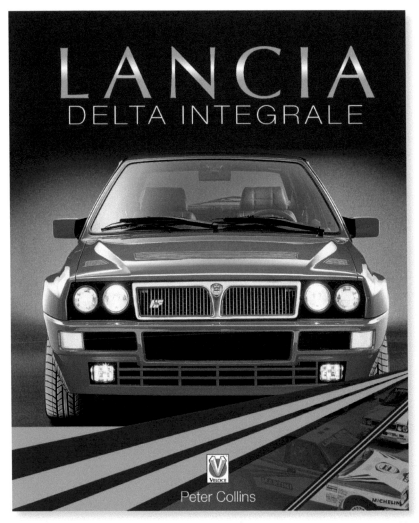

A legend on the road, race track and rally stage, the Lancia integrale was a machine to be reckoned with during its heyday in the 1980s. This book tells the full story of this much sought-after car.

ISBN: 978-1-787110-76-2
Hardback • 25x20.7cm • 160 pages • 236 pictures
Also available as an ebook.

Index

Notes

Jaguar World Monthly
An excellent independent monthly magazine by Kelsey Publishing (www.jaguar-world.com). Has regular news and features on the X300/308. Many trade advertisements and includes American pages with adverts relevant to the USA.

The on-line X300 Book
Author: Various contributors. Available to read for free at https://www.jag-lovers.com/models/x300/ and extremely useful for most systems. Best downloaded complete and then printed in sections as and when required.

The XJ-S Book
Author: Kirbert Palm and contributors. Another free download from Jag-Lovers and regarded by many as the definitive collection of all things V12, at least in terms of the engine itself. Written for the XJ-S rather than the X305, but useful for learning about V12 engine despite little specific X305 information.

Jaguar XJ-S, The Essential Buyers Guide
Author: Peter Crespin. A practical and highly-illustrated hands-on guide, to take you step-by-step through examination and purchase of Jaguar's longest-running production car of all – the legendary XJ-S Grand Tourer. Covering all engine and body configurations, this book shows what to look for, what to avoid, and whether the car is likely to suit your needs, plus relative values and the best places to buy.

Jaguar XJ-S
Author: Brian Long. The definitive history of Jaguar's E-Type replacement, the XJ-S. More a grand tourer than a sportscar, the controversially styled XJ-S offered a combination of supercar performance and grand tourer luxury. Includes rare photos of the prototypes that didn't make production.

Haynes manuals:
There are no Haynes manuals for any of the cars covered in this book. The closest, which covers similar suspension, fuelling and body systems for the normally-aspirated models is the XJ40 manual:

Jaguar XJ6 & Sovereign Oct 86-Sept 94 & Service and Repair Manual (#3621)
ISBN 1859602614
Author: Mike Stubblefield
Hardback: c.200pp

Jaguar & Daimler 12-cylinder Owners Workshop Manual
ISBN 1850102775
Author: Peter G Strasman
Hardback: 410pp
Good practical guide, not really for the XJ305 but many similarities with the 6.0L engine used.

17 Vital statistics
– essential data at your fingertips

X300/X305 production (Jaguar, Daimler/VDP combined)

Normally aspirated	Supercharged	6.0 V12	Total*
81,326	6547	4165	92,038

*Around 2% of 6-cylinder cars were manuals.

X308 production 97-2002 (Jaguar, Daimler/VDP combined)

Normally aspirated	Supercharged	Total
107,726	18,534	126,260

The above numbers are provided with grateful thanks to Anders Ditlev Clausager, Chief Archivist at the Jaguar Daimler Heritage Trust in Coventry.

Technical specifications by model
Specifications changed between years, models and markets, so only an indicative summary is possible here. Please check the appropriate information for specific models/years and markets from other sources, such as original brochures found at www.jag-lovers.org

X300 – produced 1994.5-1997.5
3.2: Inline 6-cylinder 24V DOHC, 3239 cm³, 91 x 83mm, 216bhp @ 5100rpm & 232lb/ft @ 4500rpm
4.0: Inline 6-cylinder 24V DOHC, 3980cm³, 91 x 102mm, 245bhp @ 4800rpm & 289lb/ft @ 4000rpm (XJR:322bhp @ 5000rpm & 378lb/ft @ 3050rpm)
6.0: ('94.5-96) V12 cylinder SOHC, 5993cm³, 90 x 78.5mm, 313bhp @ 5350rpm & 353lb/ft @ 2850rpm

X308 – produced 1997.5-2003.5
3.2: V8 cylinder 32V DOHC, 3248cm³, 86 x 70mm, 240bhp @ 6350rpm & 233lb/ft @ 4350rpm
4.0: V8 cylinder 32V DOHC, 3996cm³, 86 x 86mm, 290bhp @ 6100rpm & 290lb/ft @ 4250rpm (XJR: 370bhp @ 6150rpm & 387lb/ft @ 3600rpm)

All models
Transmission
Manual 6-cyl: Getrag 290 5-speed overdrive gearbox. Twin-mass flywheel.
Automatic 6-cyl: ZF 4-speed, with electronic mode selection on 4.0L models.
Automatic 6-cyl Supercharged and V12: GM 4L80E 4-speed electronic mode selection. on 4.0L models
Automatic V8: Electronic 5-speed with electronic mode selection.

Length: 16ft 5.8in (5024mm). width (inc. mirrors): 6ft 9.7in (2074mm).
Height: 4ft 3.7in (1314mm)
Weight: 3968-4354lb/1800-1974kg depending on model.

Suspension: Fully independent unequal length wishbone at the front, incorporating anti-dive geometry and mounted on a rubber-isolated subframe with anti-roll bar. Independent rear suspension, with a lower wishbone and upper driveshaft link, using a single coil spring/damper unit per side. CATS adaptive damping on some models.

Brakes: ABS ventilated power-assisted outboard disc brakes at each corner, with ABS on almost all models.

Steering: Variable power-assisted, with tilt/telescopic column. 16in wheels on most models with 17in on supercharged X300 and some V8 designs. 18in on V8 supercharged models.

The Essential Buyer's Guide™ series ...

For more details visit: www.veloce.co.uk
email: info@veloce.co.uk
tel: 01305 260068

Also from Veloce Publishing ...

ISBN: 978-1-845848-10-1
Hardback • 23.5x17cm
• 392 pages • 700 colour
and b&w pictures

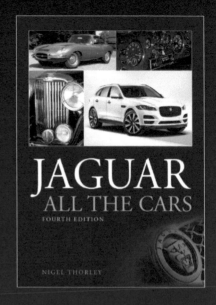

JAGUAR
All The Cars
Nigel Thorley

This significantly enhanced Fourth Edition of *Jaguar – All The Cars*, brings the Jaguar model story right up-to-date. The only publication available covering the entire range in precise detail, with a revised engine chapter, updated chapters on existing models, and new chapters on the very latest Jaguar models.